ABC Activity Book

Scott Foresman

Science

The Diamond Edition

PEARSON Scott Foresman

Editorial Offices: Glenview, Illinois • Parsippany, New Jersey • New York, New York
Sales Offices: Boston, Massachusetts • Duluth, Georgia • Glenview, Illinois
Coppell, Texas • Ontario, California • Mesa, Arizona

www.pearsonsuccessnet.com

To the Teacher

In the Scott Foresman Science ABC Activity Book, the letters of the alphabet are used to present important kindergarten-level science concepts. From *A*, which looks at Animals, through *Z*, which focuses on Zoos, the ABC Activity Book gives the alphabet a scientific slant.

For each letter and its related science concept, four cross-curricular activities are provided on a two-page spread. The first activity is always Science and has a strong focus on the science concept. The other three activities may be Science, Social Studies, Math, Reading, Writing, Art, Music, or Health. These activities are also related to the science concept. Each set of activities is supported by alphabet pages and worksheets.

Each letter has an alphabet page, which presents pictures whose names begin with that letter. Both the pictures and the words are shown on the page. The alphabet page may be used either to introduce a letter to children or to reinforce their understanding of a letter, before they complete the cross-curricular activities. The alphabet pages begin on page 54 of the ABC Activity Book and are referenced at the beginning of each letter's cross-curricular activities.

The worksheets are an integral part of the cross-curricular activities in which they are featured. They ask children to circle, color, draw pictures, cut out and paste names, match items, and write words and numbers, among other things. The worksheets begin on page 80 of the ABC Activity Book and are referenced in the Materials section of their corresponding activity. The answer keys for the worksheets are provided at the back of the book, beginning on page 147.

ISBN-13: 978-0-328-30508-7
ISBN-10: 0-328-30508-1

Copyright © Pearson Education, Inc.
All Rights Reserved. Printed in the United States of America. This publication is protected by Copyright, and permission should be obtained from the publisher prior to any prohibited reproduction, storage in a retrieval system, or transmission in any form by any means, electronic, mechanical, photocopying, recording, or otherwise. For information regarding permission(s), write to: Permissions Department, Scott Foresman, 1900 East Lake Avenue, Glenview, Illinois 60025.

5 6 7 8 9 10 V036 16 15 14 13 12 11 10 09

© Pearson Education, Inc. K

Table of Contents

© Pearson Education, Inc. K

Animals

Use the worksheet on page 54 to introduce the letter A.

Science

What Animals Need

Objective: Identify things animals need to live.

Science Inquiry Skills: identify, collect data, record

Materials
- crayons or markers
- copies of What Animals Need worksheet, page 80

Grouping whole group

Time 20 minutes

- Show picture cards of various animals or have children brainstorm a list of different animals. Write their answers on the board. Have children tell what they know about each animal, such as what it eats, where it gets water, and where it lives or gets shelter.
- Continue with several more examples. Then distribute the crayons and copies of the worksheet. Have children choose an animal and write the type of animal or draw a picture of it in the first box in the row.
- Ask children to complete the row by drawing pictures to show how their animal gets water and food, and where it might live or get shelter.
- Have children share their charts with the class.

Music

Sing an Animal Song

Objective: Tell about an animal in a song.

Science Inquiry Skills: observe, identify, communicate

Grouping whole group

Time 15 minutes

- Teach children the song "Hunky Chunky Elephant" sung to the tune of "Itsy Bitsy Spider."
- Guide children to make the appropriate movements as they sing the song.
- Change the words to the song. Have children sing about another animal. Have them move like the animal as they sing the song.

Hunky Chunky Elephant

The hunky chunky
elephant sprayed
water in the air.
He soaked all his
friends and didn't
even care.
Out came the Sun and
dried up all the spray,
And the hunky chunky
elephant will spray
again today.

© Pearson Education, Inc. K

Writing

Our Favorite Animals

Objective: Complete a sentence about an animal.

Science Inquiry Skills: identify, communicate

Materials
- pencils
- crayons or markers
- copies of My Favorite Animal worksheet, page 81

Grouping whole group

Time 20 minutes

- Ask children to name their favorite animal. Make a list of the animals they name on the board.
- Write the following sentence frame on the board: *This is a* ___. Read the sentence frame aloud to children.
- Distribute copies of the worksheet.
- Ask children to complete the sentence by writing the name of their favorite animal on the lines. Then have them draw a picture in the box to match their sentence.
- Allow time for children to read their sentences aloud and share their pictures with the group. Then collect the worksheets and create a class book titled *Our Favorite Animals.*

Social Studies

Animals Around the World

Objective: Identify places where animals live.

Science Inquiry Skills: identify, collect data, communicate

Materials
- crayons or markers
- copies of Animals Around the World worksheet, page 82

Grouping whole group

Time 15 minutes

- Show children a picture of an elephant. Tell children that an elephant is a wild animal. Then display a world map and point to the continent of Africa. Explain that many elephants live on the grasslands in Africa. Describe to children what a grassland habitat is like.
- Continue with other animals and their habitats. (Monkey, parrot, jaguar—rain forest; whale, dolphin, octopus, shark—oceans; polar bear, penguin, caribou—tundra; giraffe, lion, rhinoceros, zebra—grasslands; owl, deer, bear, squirrel—forests; gila monster, lizard, rattlesnake, roadrunner—deserts). Use the map to point to examples of locations around the world of each habitat.
- Distribute the crayons and copies of the worksheet.
- Ask children to draw a wild animal. Then help them circle the habitat where that animal lives.
- Allow time for children to show their pictures and tell where the animals live.

© Pearson Education, Inc. K

Body Parts

Use the worksheet on page 55 to introduce the letter B.

Science

Name That Body Part

Objective: Identify and locate parts of the body.

Science Inquiry Skills: identify, collect data, record

Materials
- word cards: head, neck, arm, leg, foot, hand, eye, nose, mouth, ear
- pencils
- pocket chart
- copies of Name That Body Part worksheet, page 83

Grouping whole group

Time 20 minutes

- Name a body part. Have children point to the body part you named on their body.
- Show the word card and read the word. Have children name the letters in the word.
- Repeat with the other word cards. Then place the word cards for head, leg, and arm in a pocket chart.
- Distribute copies of the worksheet. Have children write the word for each body part on the lines using the words in the pocket chart as models.

Health

A Healthy Body

Objective: Identify what people can do to keep healthy.

Science Inquiry Skills: identify, communicate

Materials
- *Bunny Day* by Rick Walton
- copies of A Healthy Body worksheet, page 84

Grouping whole group

Time 15 minutes

- Display *Bunny Day* and picture walk through the book. Ask children to describe the illustrations and actions of the bunnies.
- Read *Bunny Day*. Ask: ***What are some things the bunnies did to be healthy?*** Lead children to determine that the bunnies ate healthy foods, exercised, rested, and cleaned their bodies.
- Tell children that you are going to describe a situation; they should tell which is the healthy choice. Say: ***Listen carefully. I like to have a snack after school. Should I have an apple or cookies?*** Continue with examples of resting, exercising, and cleanliness.
- Distribute copies of the worksheet. Read aloud the heading in each row. Discuss the pictures with children. Then ask them to circle the healthy choice.

© Pearson Education, Inc. K

Music

The Body Parts Song

Objective: Identify and locate parts of the body using a song.

Science Inquiry Skills: observe, identify, communicate

Grouping whole group

Time 15 minutes

- Teach children the song "Head and Shoulders, Knees and Toes," sung to the tune of "London Bridge Is Falling Down."
- Have children point to the appropriate body parts as they sing each verse of the song.
- Point out that this song is a great way to get some healthy exercise.

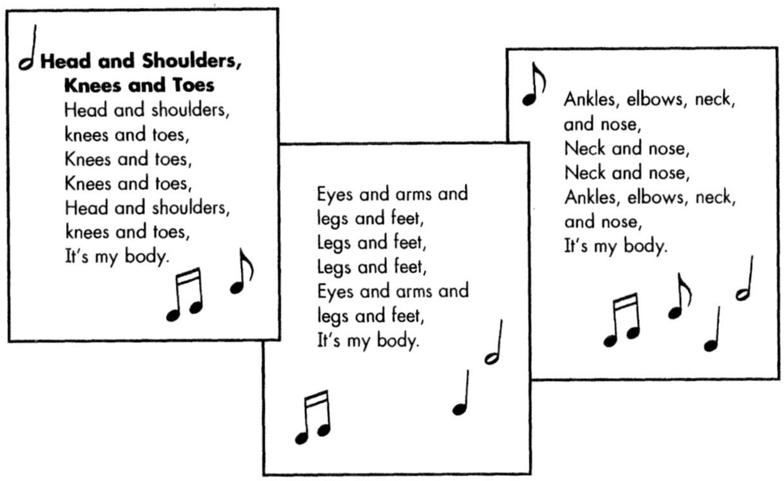

Writing

Tell About Me

Objective: Complete a sentence describing oneself.

Science Inquiry Skills: identify, communicate

Materials
- pencils
- crayons or markers
- copies of Tell About Me worksheet, page 85

Grouping whole group

Time 20 minutes

- Ask children to use describing words to tell about themselves. Offer an example about yourself: *I have red hair.* List the words children give on the board.
- Write the following sentence frame on the board: *I* ___.
  Read the sentence frame aloud to children.
- Distribute copies of the worksheet.
- Ask children to complete the sentence by writing a word from the list on the line. Then have them draw a picture in the box to go with their sentence.
- Allow time for children to share their sentences and pictures with the group.

© Pearson Education, Inc. K

Change and Grow

Use the worksheet on page 56 to introduce the letter C.

Science

A Butterfly's Life

Objective: Find out how one animal changes as it grows.

Science Inquiry Skills: identify, collect data, record

Materials
- pictures of the four stages in the life cycle of a butterfly
- crayons or pencils
- copies of A Butterfly's Life worksheet, page 86

Grouping whole group

Time 20 minutes

- Talk with children about the four stages of a butterfly's life—egg, caterpillar, pupa, butterfly. You may wish to draw simple drawings.
- Ask children to tell how the animal changes—What does it look like as it goes through each stage of its life cycle?
- Distribute copies of the worksheet.
- Have children number the pictures to show the correct order of the stages in a butterfly's life cycle.

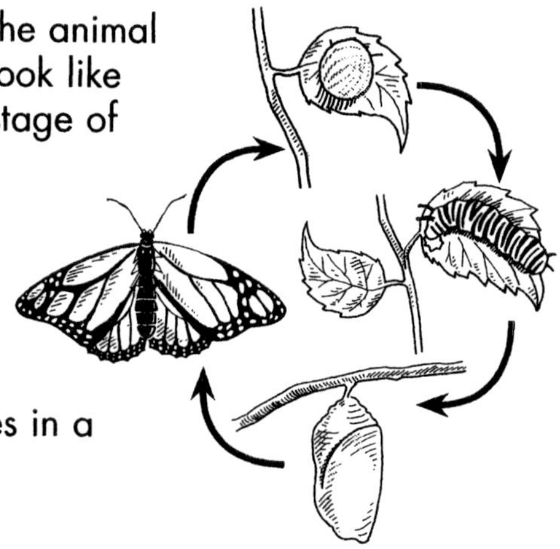

Reading

How We Change and Grow

Objective: Recognize how people change as they grow.

Science Inquiry Skills: identify, communicate

Materials
- crayons or pencils
- copies of Change and Grow worksheet, page 87

Grouping whole group

Time 15 minutes

- Discuss with children different ways they have changed since they were a baby.
- On chart paper draw two large boxes. Label the top box *Then* and the bottom box *Now.* In the top box write this sentence: *I crawled.* In the bottom box write this sentence: *I walk.* Read both sentences with children.

- Distribute copies of the worksheet.
- Ask children to complete the sentences by writing words on the lines or drawing pictures in the boxes. Help them with any words they want to write.
- Collect the papers and compile them into a class book. Encourage children take turns reading the book aloud.

© Pearson Education, Inc. K

Science — Little to Big

Objective: Understand that baby animals become adult animals.

Science Inquiry Skills: identify, communicate

Materials
- pictures of a puppy, a chick, a bear cub, a fawn, a kitten, and a duckling
- crayons or markers
- copies of Little to Big worksheet, page 88

Grouping pairs

Time 15 minutes

- Show the picture of a puppy. Guide children to describe how the puppy will change as it grows up and what it will grow up to be. *(dog)*
- Continue with the pictures of the chick *(hen* or *rooster),* cub *(bear),* fawn *(deer),* kitten *(cat),* and duckling *(duck).*
- Distribute copies of the worksheet.
- Have children work in pairs. Ask children to draw a line to match each baby animal with the correct grown-up animal. Then have children color the animals.
- Ask children how they matched the pairs of animals and how the animals change as they grow.

Math — First, Second, Third

Objective: Identify what comes first, second, and third.

Science Inquiry Skills: observe, identify

Materials
- pictures of seeds, a tiny seedling, and a full-grown plant; an egg, a chick, and a hen; a baby, a child, and an adult
- index cards labeled 1, 2, 3
- pocket chart

Grouping whole group

Time 15 minutes

- Place the numbered index cards in the bottom row of a pocket chart with space between them. Place the pictures of the seedling, the plant, and the seeds, in that order, in the top row.
- Ask children to describe the three pictures. Have them decide which comes first, second, and third.
- Have a volunteer place the number cards under the picture cards to show the correct order.

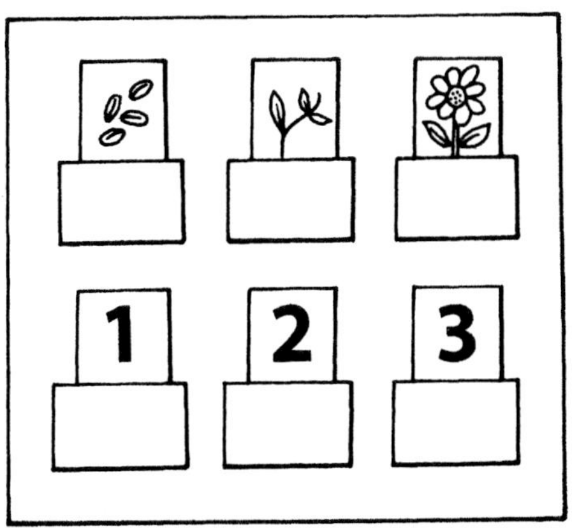

- Continue with the other two sets of pictures.
- When all three sets of pictures are in order, point to each picture in a set and have children complete these sentences: *The ___ is first. The ___ is second. The ___ is third.*

© Pearson Education, Inc. K

Day and Night

Use the worksheet on page 57 to introduce the letter D.

Science

Day to Night, Night to Day

Objective: Model how the Sun and the Earth's movement cause day and night.

Science Inquiry Skills: model, infer, communicate

Materials
- flashlight
- globe
- copies of Day to Night, Night to Day worksheet, page 89

Grouping whole group

Time 20 minutes

- Display a globe. Point out your town on Earth and attach a small sticker to that spot.
- Have one child hold the flashlight and shine it toward the globe at waist level. Have another child hold the globe with the sticker pointing toward the flashlight.
- Ask the child with the globe to rotate it slowly. Tell children it is daytime *when the "Sun" is shining on the sticker* and night *when* the "Sun" is not shining on the sticker.
- Distribute copies of the worksheet. Write the words *day* and *night* on the board. Have children write the words on the appropriate lines in each diagram.

Art

Day or Night?

Objective: Describe what day and night look like.

Science Inquiry Skills: observe, identify, communicate

Materials
- crayons or markers
- copies of Day or Night? worksheet, page 90

Grouping individuals

Time 15 minutes

- Have children describe the day and night sky. Then have them compare and contrast the day and night sky. You may wish to display pictures from books.
- Divide children into two groups. Distribute the Day or Night? worksheet. Have half of the class draw pictures of what you might see in the day sky. Have the other children draw the night sky.
- Have children title their picture, Day or Night. Have them circle words at the bottom of the page that tell about their picture.
- When finished, ask children to hold up their picture if you name something that could be seen in the sky at the time of their picture. For example, hold up your picture if the Sun is shining brightly or hold up your picture if stars are shining brightly. Continue with other examples that distinguish the day and night sky.

© Pearson Education, Inc. K

Writing

Day Sky, Night Sky

Objective: Complete sentences about what might be seen in the day sky and the night sky.

Science Inquiry Skills: identify, communicate

Materials
- pencils
- crayons or markers
- copies of Day Sky, Night Sky worksheet, page 91

Grouping individuals

Time 15 minutes

- Ask children to think of things they might see in the sky during the day. List their ideas on the board. *(Sun, clouds, plane, birds)*
- Write the following sentence frame on the board: *I see* ___. Read the sentence frame aloud to children.
- Distribute copies of the Day Sky, Night Sky worksheet.
- Ask children to complete the sentence by writing one of the words on the lines. Have them illustrate the sentence.

- Repeat the activity using the same sentence frame. Ask children to name things they might see in the sky at night. *(Moon, stars, clouds, plane)* Have them complete the sentence again and draw another picture.

Music

Day and Night Song

Objective: Identify the major features of the day sky and the night sky using a song.

Science Inquiry Skills: identify, communicate

Grouping whole group

Time 15 minutes

- Teach children the "Day and Night Song," sung to the tune of "The Farmer in the Dell."
- As the children sing the song, encourage them to emphasize the words *Sun, day, Moon,* and *night.*

Day and Night Song
Oh, do you see the Sun?
Oh, do you see the Sun?
Hi ho the derry-o,
The day has now begun.

Oh, do you see the Moon?
Oh, do you see the Moon?
Hi ho the derry-o,
The night will be here soon.

© Pearson Education, Inc. K

Earth

Use the worksheet on page 58 to introduce the letter E.

Science — Earth's Dirt

Objective: Learn about the soil that makes up the Earth.

Science Inquiry Skills: observe, identify, communicate

Materials
- *Dirt* by Steve Tomecek (or another book about dirt)
- copies of Wonderful, Marvelous Dirt! worksheet, page 92

Grouping whole group

Time 20 minutes

- Draw a KWL chart on the board. Ask children to tell you what they know about dirt. List children's responses under the *K* portion of the chart. Then ask what they would like to know about dirt, and list those responses under the *W* portion of the chart.
- Read aloud the book *Dirt.*
- After reading, ask children to name things they learned about dirt. List their responses under the *L* portion of the chart. Review the chart. Lead children to determine that dirt is one of the most important things on Earth.
- Distribute copies of the worksheet. Have children illustrate one fact they learned about dirt. Then have them write or dictate a sentence describing the illustration.

Reading — Earthworms

Objective: Identify animals that live in the ground.

Science Inquiry Skills: identify, communicate

Materials
- *Diary of a Worm* by Doreen Cronin (or another book about worms)
- copies of Earthworms worksheet, page 93
- pencils and crayons

Grouping whole group

Time 20 minutes

- Display *Diary of a Worm.* Read the title to children and explain what a diary is and how people use them. Ask children to predict what the book will be about.
- Read *Diary of a Worm.* After reading, ask children to retell the story by recalling the worm's diary entries.
- Ask children to explain how worms help the flowers and plants to grow.
- Distribute copies of the Earthworms worksheet. Ask children to complete the booklet by writing about their own worm. When children are finished, help them cut the pages of the booklet out and staple it together.

© Pearson Education, Inc. K

Math

Earth Rocks!

Objective: Count and sort rocks.

Science Inquiry Skills:
identify, classify, communicate

Materials
- sets of 10 rocks in two sizes, big and little
- index cards
- pencils
- copies of Earth Rocks! worksheet, page 94

Grouping small groups

Time 15 minutes

- Divide the class into small groups. Give each group 10 rocks and four index cards.
- Have groups divide their rocks into four sets of one, two, three, and four rocks. They can check their work by counting the rocks in each set and writing the number on a card. Have them use the cards to label the sets of rocks.
- Then have groups mix their rocks and sort them into two sets—one set of big and one set of little rocks. Talk with them about how they decided which rocks belonged in each set.
- Distribute copies of the Earth Rocks! worksheet. Have children count the rocks in each picture and write the number on the lines. Then ask them to color only the big rocks in the pictures.

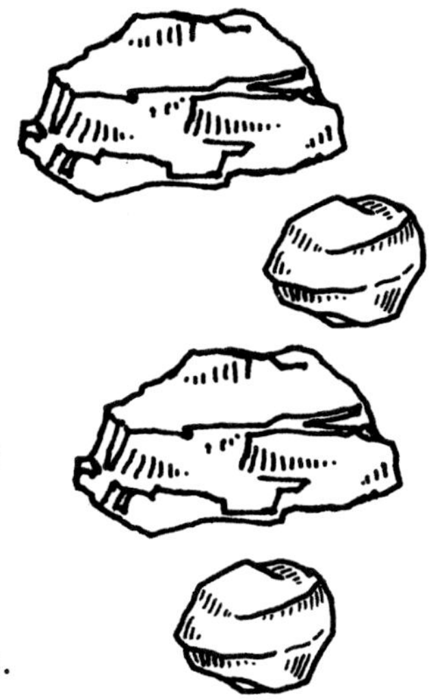

Social Studies

Water on Earth

Objective: Identify the kinds of water on Earth.

Science Inquiry Skills:
observe, identify, communicate

Materials
- globe

Grouping whole group

Time 15 minutes

- Have children brainstorm different kinds of water. Write their answers on the board.
- Show children the globe. Tell children that the blue means water. Point out different examples of water. Be sure children understand that most of Earth is covered with water.

© Pearson Education, Inc. K

Fast or Slow? Loud or Soft?

Use the worksheet on page 59 to introduce the letter F.

Science

Is It Fast or Slow?

Objective: Recognize the difference between fast and slow movements.

Science Inquiry Skills: identify, collect data, record

Materials
- ball
- crayons or markers
- copies of Is It Fast or Slow? worksheet, page 95

Grouping whole group

Time 20 minutes

- Sit with children in a circle on the floor. Display a ball and ask how you can make it move. Then roll the ball slowly to a child. Ask children whether the ball moved fast or slow. *(slow)*
- Have the child with the ball roll it quickly to another child. Ask children whether the ball moved fast or slow. *(fast)* Continue to take turns rolling the ball quickly and slowly to one another.
- Ask children to name fast things and slow things.
- Distribute copies of the Is It Fast or Slow? worksheet. Ask children to draw pictures of things that are fast in the *Fast* column and things that are slow in the *Slow* column of the chart.

Science

Is It Loud or Soft?

Objective: Recognize the difference between loud and soft sounds.

Science Inquiry Skills: identify, communicate

Materials
- *The Wheels on the Bus* by Raffi
- crayons
- copies of Is It Loud or Soft? worksheet, page 96

Grouping whole group

Time 20 minutes

- Display *The Wheels on the Bus.* Ask children to predict what will happen in the book. Then read *The Wheels on the Bus.*
- Ask children to name some of the noises heard on the bus. Then ask: Which noises on the bus were loud? Which noises were soft?
- Tell children that you are going to name two things that make sound, and that they should tell you which sound is loud and which is soft. Say: ***Listen carefully: a bird and a bulldozer; a bumblebee and a dog.*** Continue with other examples.
- Distribute copies of the worksheet. Read aloud the heading at the top of each column. Ask children to circle the items in the loud column that make a loud noise. Then circle the items in the soft column that make a soft noise.

© Pearson Education, Inc. K

Math

Which Is Faster?

Objective: Compare speeds and identify the number that is faster.

Science Inquiry Skills: identify, communicate

Materials
- pictures of a car, bike, airplane, train, boat, hot-air balloon, horse
- crayons
- copies of Which Is Faster? worksheet, page 97

Grouping small groups

Time 15 minutes

- Gather pictures of different forms of transportation, such as a car, bike, airplane, train, boat, hot-air balloon, and a horse.
- Display a picture of a bike and a car. Ask children whether they would get to the store faster if they rode a bike or rode in a car. *(car)* Why?
- Display a picture of a train and an airplane. Ask which one is faster. Continue to display different pairs of pictures and ask children to determine which is faster.

- Distribute copies of Which Is Faster? worksheet. Ask children to compare the two pictures and color the picture that shows something that moves faster.

Music

Sing Loud and Soft

Objective: Make fast and slow actions and loud and soft sounds in a song.

Science Inquiry Skills: identify, communicate

Grouping whole group

Time 15 minutes

- Teach children this revised version of the song "This Old Man."
- Point out that in the first verse children are to tap softly and walk slowly. In second verse they are to tap loudly and walk quickly.

This Old Man

This old man, he tapped one,
He tapped *soft* sounds on my thumb,
With a knick-knack, patty-whack,
Give the dog a bone!
Slow is how the man walked home.

This old man, he tapped two,
He tapped *loud* sounds on my shoe,
With a knick-knack, patty-whack,
Give the dog a bone!
Fast is how the man walked home.

© Pearson Education, Inc. K

Gases, Liquids, Solids

Use the worksheet on page 60 to introduce the letter G.

Science

What Is It?

Objective: Identify gases, liquids, and solids.

Science Inquiry Skills: model, infer, communicate

Materials
- balloon filled with air
- bottle of water
- large book
- glue
- copies of What Is It? worksheet, page 98

Grouping whole group

Time 20 minutes

- Display an air-filled balloon, a bottle of water, and a book. Ask children to point out the liquid. *(the water)* Remind them that a liquid is something that takes the shape of its container, just as the water takes the shape of the bottle.
- Ask children to point out the gas. *(the air in the balloon)* Let them squeeze the balloon so they can feel the air in it. Remind children that a gas cannot be seen and has no shape of its own.
- Have children identify the book as a solid because it keeps its shape.
- Distribute copies of the What Is It? worksheet. Ask children to color the pictures and then cut them out. Have children glue each picture in the appropriate box.

Art

They're a Gas!

Objective: Demonstrate how gas can take up space.

Science Inquiry Skills: observe, identify, communicate

Materials
- balloon

Grouping whole group

Time 10 minutes

- Draw a face with a marker on a deflated balloon.
- Show children the blank side of the balloon. Ask children what you should do to make the balloon bigger.
- Ask children what they think will happen if you fill the balloon with a gas.
- Blow the balloon up. Tell children that you filled the balloon with a gas. Display the side of the balloon with the face. Tell children that you made a balloon person.
- Review with children that air is a gas that surrounds them. Gas has no shape or size of its own.

© Pearson Education, Inc. K

Science

Watch the Changes!

Objective: Find out how a solid can change into a liquid, a liquid can change into a solid, and a liquid can change into a gas.

Science Inquiry Skills: identify, observe, model, communicate

Materials
- small pan of water and several ice cubes on a tray
- crayons or markers
- copies of Watch the Changes! worksheet, page 99

Grouping whole group

Time 20 minutes

- Display the pan of water. Point to the water and ask children whether it is a gas, liquid, or solid. *(liquid)*
- Display the ice cubes on the tray. Point to the ice cubes and ask children whether they are a gas, liquid, or solid. *(solid)* Ask children what had to be done to the water to make it change into ice. *(It had to be frozen.)* Explain that freezing changed a liquid (water) into a solid (ice).
- Distribute copies of the Watch the Changes! worksheet. Ask children to draw pictures in the first section of the page to show the different changes they learned about in the demonstration.
- Set the tray of ice cubes in a sunny window. When they have melted into water, point out to children that melting has changed a solid (ice) into a liquid (water). Have children complete the second section of the worksheet.
- Leave the water in the window until it has evaporated. Explain to children that evaporation has changed a liquid (water) into a gas (water vapor). Have children complete the third section of the worksheet.

Music

All Steamed Up

Objective: Identify a gas, a liquid, and a solid in a song.

Science Inquiry Skills: model, infer, communicate

Materials
- crayons
- copies of All Steamed Up worksheet, page 100

Grouping whole group

Time 15 minutes

- Teach children the song "I'm a Little Teapot."
- Point out that the song tells about a teapot, the water in the teapot, and the steam that comes out of the teapot when the water is heated. Ask children which of the three things—teapot, water, steam—is a gas, a liquid, and a solid.
- Together sing and act out the song one more time.
- Distribute copies of the All Steamed Up worksheet. Have children draw lines to match pictures of the things connected with the song to the words that identify them.

I'm a Little Teapot

I'm a little teapot,
Short and stout.
Here is my handle.
Here is my spout.

When I get all
steamed up,
Then I shout,
"Just tip me over
And pour me out!"

© Pearson Education, Inc. K

Heat and Light

Use the worksheet on page 61 to introduce the letter H.

Science

What We All Need

Objective: Recognize the importance of heat and light to all living things.

Science Inquiry Skills: infer, communicate

Materials
- crayons
- copies of Heat and Light worksheet, page 101

Grouping whole group

Time 20 minutes

- Ask the following questions:
  What do you need so you won't get cold? *(heat)*
  What do you need so you aren't in the dark? *(light)*
- Ask children where heat comes from. Accept answers such as heaters, fire, and stoves. Point out that our most important source of heat is the Sun.
- Ask children where light comes from. Accept answers such as lamps, flashlights, and candles. Point out that our most important source of light is sunlight.
- Distribute copies of the Heat and Light worksheet. Read the titles in each section and have children draw pictures of sources of heat and sources of light.

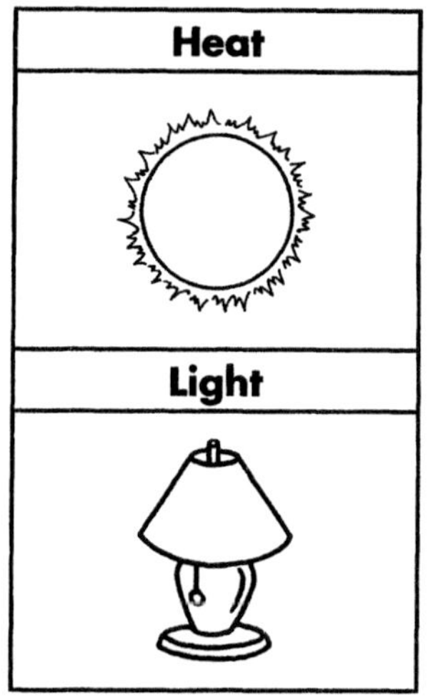

Reading

What Is the Sun?

Objective: Learn about the Sun.

Science Inquiry Skills: observe, identify, communicate

Materials
- *What Is the Sun?* by Reeve Lindbergh
- copies of The Sun worksheet, page 102

Grouping whole group

Time 15 minutes

- Display the book *What Is the Sun?* Ask children to predict what the book will be about.
- Read *What Is the Sun?*
- Ask children to answer the question, what is the Sun? List their responses.
- Distribute the worksheet. Ask children to complete the sentence starter, *The Sun is ...* . Then ask them to illustrate their sentence.
- You may wish to find information about the Sun on the Internet or in other books, if you do not have a copy of *What Is the Sun?*

© Pearson Education, Inc. K

Math

Light Count

Objective: Count things that give light.

Science Inquiry Skills:
identify, communicate

Materials
- crayons

Grouping whole group

Time 20 minutes

- Draw a chart like the one shown below on the board.
- Ask children to look around the room and find things that give light.
- List children's responses on the chart. Choose one thing that children name and count how many of this thing there are in the classroom. Write the number on the board. Ask children to read the number with you.
- Continue in the same way with the other things that children named.
- Compare and contrast their results. They may also add other items to the list.

Light	How many?

Writing

Write a Rhyme

Objective: Write words that rhyme with *heat* and *light*.

Science Inquiry Skills:
infer, communicate

Materials
- crayons or markers
- copies of Write a Rhyme worksheet, page 103

Grouping whole group

Time 15 minutes

- Write these sentences on the board:
  Where is the heat?
  It is by my ___.
- Ask children to think of a word that rhymes with *heat* and makes sense in the sentence.
- Write the word *feet* on the board. Have children read the rhyme with you. Then write these sentences:
  Look at the light.
  It is so ___!
- Have children think of a word that rhymes with *light* and makes sense in the sentence.
- Write the word *bright* on the board and read the rhyme with children.
- Distribute the crayons and copies of the Write a Rhyme worksheet. Have children complete the rhymes with the words *feet* and *bright*. Then have them draw a picture to go with each rhyme.

© Pearson Education, Inc. K

Important Inventions

Use the worksheet on page 62 to introduce the letter I.

Science

Time to Talk

Objective: Compare and contrast old and new telephones.

Science Inquiry Skills: infer, compare, communicate

Materials
- pictures or models of an early telephone and a cell phone

Grouping whole group

Time 20 minutes

- Show children pictures or models of old and new telephones. (Encyclopedias usually have pictures showing the development of the phone.) Explain that the telephone was invented in 1871, or more than 140 years ago.
- Ask children to tell why they think someone invented the telephone. *(so people could communicate over long distances)*
- Have children compare and contrast the old telephone and the new cell phone.
- Ask children to recite their home phone numbers. Point out that it is a good idea for them to know their phone numbers in case of an emergency. You may wish to teach children how to use 911.

Social Studies

How Should I Travel?

Objective: Compare and contrast ways to travel in the past and present.

Science Inquiry Skills: observe, compare, communicate

Materials
- pictures of horse and wagon, car
- crayons or markers
- copies of How Should I Travel? worksheet, page 104

Grouping whole group

Time 20 minutes

- Show the picture of a horse and wagon. Point out that two hundred years ago, this was one way that people traveled.
- Discuss with children what it would feel like to travel by horse and wagon and how long it might take to get someplace.
- Ask children how people travel today. Record their answers on the board. *(car, bus, plane, train)*
- Show the picture of the car. Have children compare traveling by horse and wagon to traveling by car. Discuss which way would be faster and which way would let people travel farther.
- Distribute copies of the worksheet. Have children draw a picture of a form of transportation they would like to use. Have them write or dictate a sentence about their picture.

© Pearson Education, Inc. K

Art — Air Travel

Objective: Make a paper airplane.

Science Inquiry Skills:
identify, communicate

Materials
- construction paper
- crayons

Grouping whole group

Time 20 minutes

- Tell children that the first airplane was invented by Orville and Wilbur Wright more than one hundred years ago. Have children tell what they know about airplanes and share any experiences they have had traveling on airplanes.
- Give each child a sheet of construction paper. Show children how to fold the top corners of the paper toward each other to form two triangles and a point at the top of the paper. Then fold the paper in half lengthwise. Finally, fold down about 1 1/2 inches of each side of the paper and spread out these parts to form wings.

- Encourage children to decorate their airplanes either before or after they fold them.
- Have children take turns flying their planes in an open area of the classroom. See how far each plane can fly.

Writing — Here Comes the Mail!

Objective: Write a message to a friend or family member.

Science Inquiry Skills:
infer, compare, communicate

Materials
- pencils or crayons
- copies of Here Comes the Mail! worksheet, page 105

Grouping individuals

Time 15 minutes

- Explain to children that people have written and sent messages to one another for thousands of years. For a brief time in the 1800s, the Pony Express delivered letters. Explain how the riders would ride horses from station to station to deliver the mail across our country.
- Ask children how letters and packages are delivered today. Discuss how today's postal service is different from the Pony Express.
- Have children think of other ways, besides letters, that people can send messages. Tell them that e-mail uses a computer and the Internet to send messages. Show examples of e-mail or use a computer to demonstrate how to write and send an e-mail message. Ask children to share their experiences with e-mail.
- Distribute copies of the worksheet. Have children write or draw a letter to send to a family member or friend.

© Pearson Education, Inc. K

Jump, Run, Walk, Move

Use the worksheet on page 63 to introduce the letter J.

Science — Ways to Move

Objective: Describe different ways that people can move.

Science Inquiry Skills: infer, compare, communicate

Materials
- crayons
- copies of Ways to Move worksheet, page 106

Grouping whole group

Time 20 minutes

- Have children form a line. Tell them to follow your directions.

  I jump, jump, jump.
  I jump and jump this way.
  I jump, jump, jump.
  This is how I move today.

- Continue the activity substituting each of the words below for the word *jump* in the directions.

sway	*hop*	*skip*
twirl	*run*	*march*
prance	*tiptoe*	*slide*

- Distribute copies of the Ways to Move worksheet. Read the sentences together. Then have children circle the sentence that tells how the child in each row is moving.

Health — Let's Move!

Objective: Understand that physical exercise is important for good health.

Science Inquiry Skills: observe, communicate

Grouping whole group

Time 15 minutes

- Explain to children that exercise is anything we do to make our bodies move and that exercise is important because it helps us stay healthy. Ask children what activities they do to get exercise.
- Teach children the "Exercise Song," sung to the tune of "Here We Go 'Round the Mulberry Bush." Have children do the exercise as they sing the verse.

Exercise Song

This is the way we touch our toes,
Touch our toes, touch our toes.
This is the way we touch our toes,
So we get good exercise.
This is the way we stretch our arms,
Stretch our arms, stretch our arms.
This is the way we stretch our arms,
So we get good exercise.

© Pearson Education, Inc. K

Music

Musical Movements

Objective: Demonstrate how people move to music.

Science Inquiry Skills: identify, communicate

Materials
- different kinds of music to play

Grouping whole group

Time 20 minutes

- Have children listen as you play music. Play a march, such as one by John Philip Sousa. Ask children what kinds of movements the music makes them feel like doing. Encourage them to show how they would move. Suggest that the music is perfect for marching.
- Stop the music and let children practice how they will march. Then have them form a line. Play the march again as they march around the room.
- Continue with the other kinds of music you select. You might use ballet music for twirling and spinning, rap music for slides and bends, or pop music for hops and twists.

Reading

Action Words

Objective: Practice reading and using action words.

Science Inquiry Skills: identify, communicate

Materials
- word cards: jump, run, walk, hop, skip, spin, turn, march
- crayons
- copies of Action Words worksheet, page 107
- pocket chart

Grouping individuals

Time 20 minutes

- Place the word cards in a pocket chart. Have a child demonstrate the action that goes with one of the words. Then have the class figure out which word the child is acting out. Then say the word.
- Continue in the same way with the other word cards until all the words have been read and demonstrated.
- Distribute copies of the worksheet. Assign one of the action words to each child. Have children draw a picture that shows someone doing that action and label their picture by writing the action word on the lines.
- Let children share their pictures with the class.
- Compile the pages to make a class book titled *Action Words*.

© Pearson Education, Inc. K

Kinds of Habitats and Homes

Use the worksheet on page 64 to introduce the letter K.

Science

Where Is My Home?

Objective: Understand that habitats are places where plants and animals live.

Science Inquiry Skills: infer, communicate

Materials
- *Animal Homes* by Angela Wilkes (or a similar book)
- copies of Where Is My Home? worksheet, page 108

Grouping whole group

Time 15 minutes

- Display the book *Animal Homes*. Build oral vocabulary by naming the animals as you picture walk through the book. Encourage children to share what they know about some of the animals.
- Read *Animal Homes*. Remind children that animals have homes to keep them safe. Animal homes are often called *habitats*.
- Randomly open to a page. Ask children to describe the habitat pictured. Ask children to tell what makes the home unique but appropriate for that particular animal. Have children name other plants and animals that also live in the habitat. You may wish to list children's responses with words and simple illustrations.
- Distribute copies of Where Is My Home? worksheet. Ask children to draw a line from each animal to its home.

Social Studies

Homes for People

Objective: Discuss places where people live.

Science Inquiry Skills: observe, classify, identify, communicate

Materials
- pictures of homes for people—house, apartment building, trailer, cabin, tent—and homes for animals—nest, fishbowl, doghouse, barn

Grouping whole group

Time 15 minutes

- Show the picture of a nest. Ask children what lives in a nest. Ask them where a nest is found and if they have seen one in their neighborhood.
- Show the picture of an apartment building. Ask children to tell what it is and if there are apartment buildings in their neighborhood.
- Continue in the same way with the other pictures. Have children choose the homes for people and arrange them in a pocket chart.

© Pearson Education, Inc. K

Math

Over in the Meadow

Objective: Recognize the meadow as a habitat for animals.

Science Inquiry Skills: identify, communicate

Materials
- *Over in the Meadow* by Olive Wadsworth (or another version)
- copies of Over in the Meadow worksheet, page 109
- a strip of 6" x 18" construction paper for each child
- scissors
- glue
- crayons

Grouping whole group

Time 15 minutes

- Display the cover of *Over in the Meadow*. Tell children this is a poem written a long time ago. Many different illustrators have created illustrations for the poem.
- Tell children that the animals in the poem all live in the meadow. The meadow is a grassy habitat often found near farming areas.
- Read *Over in the Meadow*. Encourage children to participate by chiming in as you read. You may wish to reread the book.
- After reading, page through the book animal by animal. Ask children to count the animals and describe each animal's home.
- Distribute copies of Over in the Meadow worksheet and a strip of construction paper to each child. Ask children to color and cut out the animals and glue them in numerical order on the construction paper strip.
- Encourage children to retell the nursery rhyme using their animal strip as a guide.

Music

Do You Know?

Objective: Discuss places where animals and people live.

Science Inquiry Skills: identify, communicate

Materials
- crayons
- scissors
- tape
- copies of Finger Puppets worksheet, page 110

Grouping whole group

Time 15 minutes

- Teach children the first verse of the song "Do You Know?" sung to the tune of "Do You Know the Muffin Man?" When singing verses two through five, substitute the type of home and animal.
- After singing the song, ask children to name the habitat of each animal in the song. You may wish to share pictures of each type of home.
- Distribute copies of the Finger Puppets worksheet, page 110. Have children color and cut out the animals. Demonstrate how to make finger puppets.
- When children have finished making the finger puppets, have them use their finger puppets as they sing the song.

Do You Know?

Do you know who lives in a lodge,
Lives in a lodge, lives in a lodge?
Do you know who lives in a lodge?
Look, it's Mr. Beaver.

Verse 2: shell; Hermit Crab
Verse 3: den; Mama Bear
Verse 4: the treetops; Little Monkey
Verse 5: nest; Baby Bird

© Pearson Education, Inc. K

Lever, Pulley, Ramp, Wheel

Use the worksheet on page 65 to introduce the letter L.

Science

Simple Machines

Objective: Identify levers, pulleys, ramps, and wheels as simple machines.

Science Inquiry Skills: observe, infer, communicate

Materials
- ruler, one heavy book, one thin book, toy car, spool and string
- pictures of lever, pulley, ramp, wheel in action
- copies of Simple Machines worksheet, page 111

Grouping whole group

Time 20 minutes

- Place a heavy book at the edge of a desk. Put one end of the ruler under one end of the book. Show children how you can lift the book by pushing down on the other end of the ruler. Explain that here the ruler is working as a simple machine called a *lever.*
- Demonstrate the simple machines using the spool and string for the pulley, the two books for the ramp, and the toy car for the wheel, respectively.
- Point out that all four simple machines help us work more easily. They let us lift, raise, or move heavy things.
- Distribute copies of the Simple Machines worksheet. Read the words with children and have them identify what kind of simple machine they see in each picture. Have them match each word to the picture it names.

Music

A Song About Simple Machines

Objective: Review what a lever, pulley, ramp, and wheel can do using a song.

Science Inquiry Skills: identify, communicate

Materials
- pictures of lever, pulley, ramp, wheel

Grouping whole group

Time 15 minutes

- Show the picture of a lever. Have children identify it and tell what it does. Help them think of other levers they have seen in action—a screwdriver prying off the top of a can.
- Continue in the same way with the pictures of the pulley, ramp, and wheel.
- Teach children the song "Simple Machines" sung to the tune of "B-I-N-G-O." Encourage them to act out the appropriate motion with each verse.

Simple Machines
With this machine, I open a can,
And *lever* is its name-o.
L-E-V-E-R, L-E-V-E-R, L-E-V-E-R,
And *lever* is its name-o.

With this machine, I raise a load,
And *pulley* is its name-o.
P-U-LL-E-Y, P-U-LL-E-Y, P-U-LL-E-Y,
And *pulley* is its name-o.

With this machine, I push things up,
And *ramp* is its name-o.
R-A-M-P, R-A-M-P, R-A-M-P,
And *ramp* is its name-o.

With this machine, I make things move,
And *wheel* is its name-o.
W-H-E-E-L, W-H-E-E-L, W-H-E-E-L,
And *wheel* is its name-o.

© Pearson Education, Inc. K

Math

Wheel Count

Objective: Count and record numbers of wheels.

Science Inquiry Skills: identify, communicate

Materials
- toys with wheels
- copies of Wheel Count worksheet, page 112
- crayons or pencils

Grouping individuals

Time 15 minutes

- Hold up a toy with wheels and ask children to count the number of wheels. Write the number on the board. Review how to make the number as the children write it on paper.
- Continue with the other toys or pictures of things with different numbers of wheels.
- Distribute copies of the Wheel Count worksheet. Have children count the wheels on the object in each picture and write the number on the line.

Writing

Finish the Words

Objective: Write the names of simple machines.

Science Inquiry Skills: infer, observe, communicate

Materials
- word cards: lever, ramp, wheel, pulley
- pencils or crayons
- pocket chart
- copies of Finish the Words worksheet, page 113

Grouping whole group

Time 20 minutes

- Show the *lever* word card. Read the word with children. Have children name the letters. Review what a lever is and what it does. Then place the word card in a pocket chart. Continue with the *ramp, wheel,* and *pulley* word cards.
- Distribute copies of the Finish the Words worksheet.
- Point to clue 1 and read it to children. Ask them which word in the pocket chart goes with this clue. Point out that the first and last letters of the word, *w* and *l,* are already given.
- When children choose the word *wheel,* have them write the letters *h, e,* and *e* in the three boxes between the *w* and the *l,* one letter in a box. Review the clue and the word that children wrote in their puzzles.
- Continue in the same way with the other three clues and words.

© Pearson Education, Inc. K

Magnets

Use the worksheet on page 66 to introduce the letter M.

Science — Magnetic or Not?

Objective: Discover the kinds of objects that are attracted to magnets.

Science Inquiry Skills: observe, infer, communicate

Materials
- magnet
- magnetic objects (paper clip, nail, screw, washer, metal button, metal can)
- nonmagnetic objects (wood block, sheet of paper, plastic ruler, glove)

Grouping whole group

Time 20 minutes

- Remind children that a magnet attracts or pulls some metal objects toward it.
- Display a variety of metal and nonmetal objects. Ask children to predict which objects the magnet will pull.
- Have children take turns checking their predictions. Have them sort the objects into two groups: magnetic and nonmagnetic.
- Guide children to determine that only metal objects were attracted to the magnet.
- Leave the magnets and objects in the science center for children to explore.

Math — Magnetic Math

Objective: Count objects attracted to a magnet.

Science Inquiry Skills: identify, communicate

Materials
- crayons or pencils
- copies of Magnetic Math worksheet, page 114

Grouping whole group

Time 15 minutes

- Remind children that the paper clips are made of a metal that is attracted to magnets.
- Distribute copies of the Magnetic Math worksheet. Ask children to count all the paper clips in the two sets in the first row. Have them write the number on the lines at the end of the row. Then have them read aloud the number problem. Continue with the other rows.

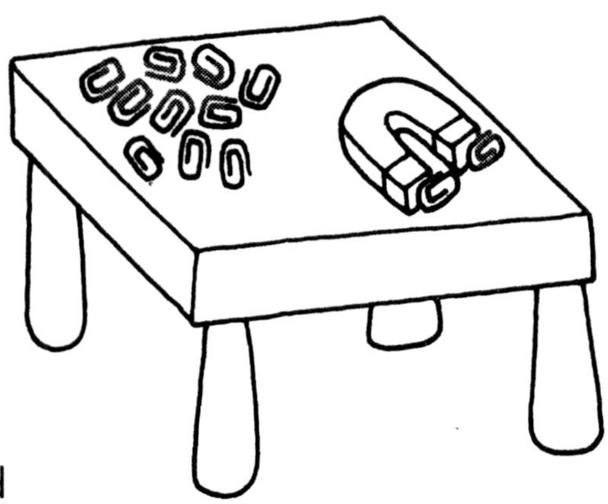

© Pearson Education, Inc. K

Science

Magnets

Objective: Discover the kinds of objects magnets will attract.

Science Inquiry Skills:
observe, communicate, infer

Materials
- *Magnets* by Becky Olien (or a similar book)
- drawing paper
- crayons or markers

Grouping individuals

Time 20 minutes

- Picture walk through *Magnets* by Becky Olien prior to reading. Build oral vocabulary by asking children to name and describe objects in the photographs.
- Read *Magnets*. Ask children to retell what they learned from each page as you reread the book.
- Ask children to share some facts they learned about magnets. List their responses on the board.
- Distribute drawing paper to each child. Ask them to draw one thing they learned about magnets. Remind them to use the list the class generated. Then have them write or dictate a sentence to describe their illustration.
- You may wish to collect the papers to create a class book about magnets.

Reading

Fishing with a Magnet

Objective: Practice reading names using a magnet game.

Science Inquiry Skills:
identify, communicate

Materials
- paper clips
- fishing pole made of a stick, a piece of string, and a magnet
- crayons
- scissors
- copies of Fishing Fun worksheet, page 115

Grouping whole group

Time 20 minutes

- Tie one end of the string to one end of the stick pole. Tie the other end of the string to the magnet. The magnet is the "hook" on the fishing pole.
- Distribute the Fishing Fun worksheet. Have each child write his or her name on the line, then color and cut out the fish. Attach a paper clip to the head of the fish.
- Place all the fish in a box. Give the fishing pole to a child. Have the child "go fishing" by dangling the magnet in the box and trying to "hook" a fish. When one fish shape sticks to the magnet, help the child read the name on the fish. Then give the fishing pole to that child to have the next turn.
- Continue until all the fish are "caught."

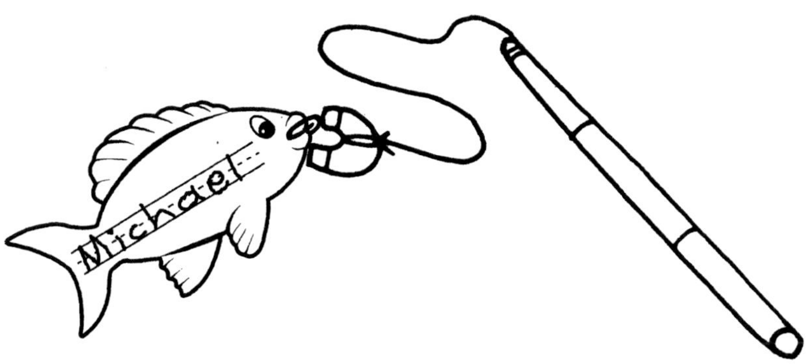

© Pearson Education, Inc. K

Nonliving and Living Things

Use the worksheet on page 67 to introduce the letter N.

Science

Nonliving or Living?

Objective: Compare and contrast nonliving and living things.

Science Inquiry Skills: observe, infer, communicate, classify

Materials
- doll, stuffed animal, classroom pet (if available)

Grouping whole group

Time 20 minutes

- Place the doll in a chair and have a child sit in another chair next to the doll. Ask children the following questions:

  Which can eat?
  Which can breathe?
  Which can move?
  Which can grow?

- Explain that because the child can eat, breathe, move, and grow, the child is living thing. Because the doll cannot do any of these things, it is a nonliving thing.
- Repeat the activity using the stuffed animal and the classroom pet.

Science

Half and Half

Objective: Identify nonliving and living things.

Science Inquiry Skills: identify, communicate, classify

Materials
- crayons or colored markers
- glue
- scissors
- copies of Nonliving or Living? worksheet, pages 116–117

Grouping whole group

Time 20 minutes

- Remind children that things that can grow and change are *living.* Things that cannot change and grow are *nonliving.*
- Ask children to look out the window and name nonliving and living things.
- Distribute the Nonliving or Living? worksheets. Hold up page 116 and name the objects with children. Then display page 117 and read the labels to children.
- Have children color and cut out the pictures on page 116. Ask them to glue each picture under the correct label on page 117.

© Pearson Education, Inc. K

Reading

What I Saw

Objective: Identify and describe nonliving and living things.

Science Inquiry Skills: identify, observe, communicate, classify

Materials
- *Duckling Days* by Karen Wallace

Grouping individuals

Time 20 minutes

- Display *Duckling Days*. Picture walk through the book. Build oral vocabulary by asking children to name objects and describe the photographs.
- Read *Duckling Days*.
- Display a toy duck. Ask children to compare and contrast the toy duck to the duck in *Duckling Days*.
- Draw a Venn diagram on the board. Fill in the diagram with children's responses.

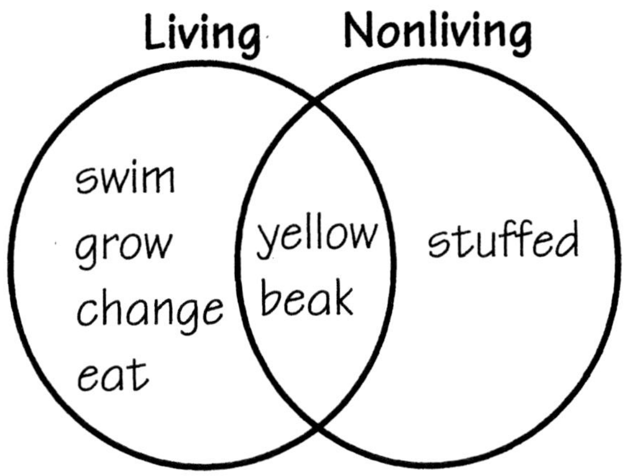

Math

Numbers of Things

Objective: Count nonliving and living things.

Science Inquiry Skills: identify, communicate, classify

Materials
- blue and red crayons
- copies of Numbers of Things worksheet, page 118

Grouping whole group

Time 15 minutes

- Distribute Number of Things worksheet. Have children describe things they see in the picture.
- Write the words *Living* and *Nonliving* on the board. Remind children that living things can eat, breathe, move, and grow, and nonliving things cannot. Ask children to name living and nonliving things in the picture.
- Distribute red and blue crayons. Ask children to circle the nonliving things with their red crayon. Then have them place an X with their blue crayon on the living things.
- When finished, ask children to count each group of nonliving things and write the numeral on the line. Repeat for living things.

© Pearson Education, Inc. K

Objects

Use the worksheet on page 68 to introduce the letter O.

Science — Group Objects

Objective: Classify objects using shape, size, color, and texture.

Science Inquiry Skills: observe, classify, infer, communicate

Materials
- large and small red, green, and blue construction paper circles, squares, and triangles
- textured paper such as sandpaper
- crayons or pencils

Grouping whole group

Time 20 minutes

- Give shapes to several children. Make sure some of the shapes have something in common. Have the children stand in a row and hold up their shapes.
- First, ask children to name each shape *(circle, square, triangle)*. Then have them tell what color each shape is. Next, ask them to tell what sizes the shapes are *(small, large)*. Finally, have them identify the ones that have the same shapes, the ones that are the same colors, and the ones that are the same sizes.
- Distribute a construction paper square and a sandpaper square. Have each child touch the surfaces of the squares. Ask children to tell which square is smooth and which is rough.

Math — Shapes on a Graph

Objective: Compare objects using a graph.

Science Inquiry Skills: identify, compare, communicate, classify

Materials
- small construction paper shapes—circle, triangle, square, rectangle
- crayons
- copies of Shapes on a Graph worksheet, page 119

Grouping whole group

Time 20 minutes

- Draw a triangle on the board. Ask children to name the shape and describe it. Continue with the other shapes—circle, square, and rectangle.
- Mix the construction paper shapes together, and then randomly distribute them to children. Each child should have several of each shape—circle, triangle, rectangle, and square, but no more than ten of one particular shape.
- Ask children to sort their objects by shape. Have them count each shape group.
- Distribute the Shapes on a Graph worksheet, page 119. Then have them fill in the graph based on the shapes they have counted.

© Pearson Education, Inc. K

Writing

Touch It!

Objective: Identify objects using texture.

Science Inquiry Skills: identify, observe, communicate

Materials
- small, deep box with hole in top large enough for hand
- several objects that have texture: fuzzy toy, bumpy sponge, smooth ribbon, rough wood block
- copies of Touch It! worksheet, page 120
- crayons or markers

Grouping individuals

Time 20 minutes

- Place all the objects into the box, making sure that children cannot see the objects.
- Distribute copies of the Touch It! worksheet and crayons.
- Hand the box to a child. The child puts one hand into the box and handles one of the objects for ten seconds. That child then passes the box to the next child and draws a picture of what he or she thinks the object is, based on how it felt.

- After all children have drawn a picture, open the box. Show one of the objects and write its name on the board. Ask who touched that object. See how many of those children correctly drew the object. Continue in the same way with the other objects in the box.
- Have children write the name—*toy, sponge, ribbon,* or *block*—of their object on the lines to complete the sentence. Suggest that if they need to, children can change their picture to match what was in the box.

Art

Object Collage

Objective: Choose and classify objects by shape, size, color, and texture.

Science Inquiry Skills: identify, observe, classify, communicate

Materials
- variety of papers, cloths, small objects
- cardboard
- glue

Grouping individuals

Time 15 minutes

- Tell children that they are going to make a collage using objects in as many different colors, shapes, sizes, and textures as they wish.
- Give each child a sheet of cardboard. Have children choose the objects they want to use in their collage.
- Have children try different arrangements of the objects. They may want to group objects with similar characteristics or mix the colors, shapes, sizes, and textures.

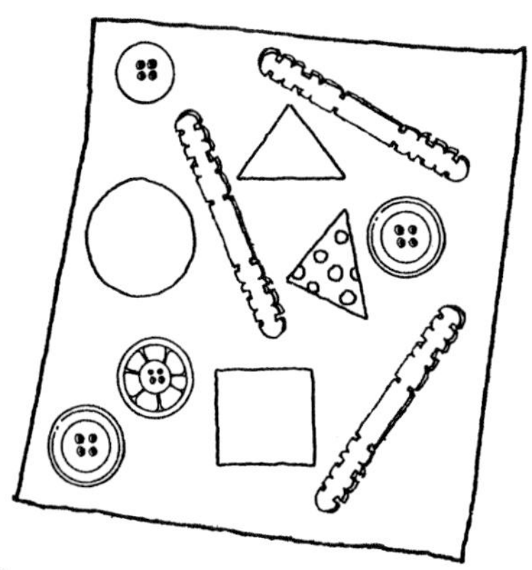

- When children have made an arrangement they like, help them glue the objects to their sheet of cardboard.
- Display children's artwork in the classroom and use it to discuss the characteristics—color, shape, size, and texture—of objects.

© Pearson Education, Inc. K

Plants

Use the worksheet on page 69 to introduce the letter P.

Science — What Plants Need

Objective: Identify things plants need to grow.

Science Inquiry Skills: identify, observe, compare

Materials
- *Growing Vegetable Soup* by Lois Ehlert
- 9" x 18" piece of construction paper for each child
- copies of How Do Plants Grow? worksheet, page 121

Grouping whole group

Time 20 minutes

- Display *Growing Vegetable Soup.* Picture walk through the book with children. Build oral vocabulary by asking children to name objects.
- Read *Growing Vegetable Soup.*
- Walk through the book again, and have children describe the sequence of growth from seed to plant. Ask them what the seeds needed to grow into plants. Record children's responses on the board.
- Distribute the worksheet. Ask children to color and then cut out the pictures. Have children glue the pictures on a piece of construction paper in the correct order. You may wish to have children review the sequence of a seed to a plant when finished.

Art — Plant Parts

Objective: Identify parts of a plant.

Science Inquiry Skills: identify, make a model

Materials
- brown and green construction paper
- brightly colored flower heads
- sheets of white construction paper

Grouping whole group

Time 20 minutes

- Draw a flower on the board. Ask children to help you label the parts of the flower.
- Model how to construct a plant using the construction paper.
- Distribute the construction paper pieces children will need to make their own flowers.
- Have children use the construction paper parts to make their plants on construction paper.
- When children are finished, help them label the four parts of the plant—roots, stem, leaves, and flower.

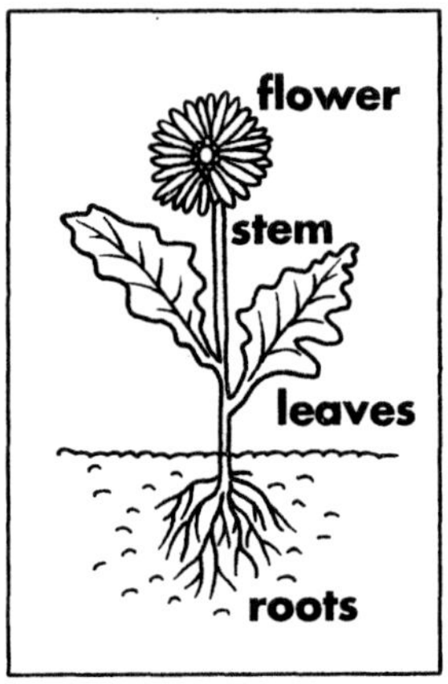

© Pearson Education, Inc. K

Math

Measure Plants

Objective: Measure plants using nonstandard units of measure.

Science Inquiry Skills: identify, observe, measure, record, communicate

Materials
- small paper clips
- crayons
- copies of Measure Plants worksheet, page 122

Grouping individuals

Time 20 minutes

- Draw a simple plant on chart paper. Make the plant seven paper clips tall. Show children how to measure the plant using paper clips. Explain that you place the end of the paper clip lined up with the bottom of the plant. Then you continue to add paper clips by placing them next to each other until you reach the top of the plant. Count the number of paper clips. Write the number of paper clips next to the plant. Ask children how many paper clips tall the plant is.

- Draw plants of other heights on chart paper and let children take turns measuring them with the paper clips.
- Distribute copies of the Measure Plants worksheet. Give each child some paper clips. Have children measure the height of each plant with paper clips and write the number of paper clips on the line.

Social Studies

Plants Around the World

Objective: Learn about the function of each part of the plant.

Science Inquiry Skills: identify, communicate

Materials
- pictures of a flower, such as a daisy
- crayons
- scissors
- stapler
- copies of Parts of a Plant worksheet, page 123

Grouping whole group

Time 15 minutes

- Draw a plant on the board. Be sure to draw the roots, stem, leaves, and flower. Ask children to name the parts of the plant.
- Point to the roots and tell children that roots take in water for the plant and hold the plant in the ground.
- Point to the stem and tell children that the stem carries water up through the plant and holds the plant up.
- Point to the leaves and tell children that the leaves take in sunlight, which the plant uses to make food.
- Point to the flower and tell children that the flower produces the seeds to make more plants. Flowers are often very colorful.
- Distribute copies of Parts of a Plant worksheet. Have children color the pictures. Have them make the child on the last page look like themselves. Next, have them cut on the dotted lines. Ask children to put the pictures in order, then staple the pages to make a book.

© Pearson Education, Inc. K

Questions

Use the worksheet on page 70 to introduce the letter Q.

Science

Begin with a Question

Objective: Discover that scientists begin by asking questions.

Science Inquiry Skills: identify, predict, infer, communicate

Grouping whole group

Time 20 minutes

- Ask children to give examples of questions. Write several of their questions on the board. Explain that questions are an important part of a scientist's job. A scientist asks a question and then tries to find the answer to the question.
- Explore ways the children find answers to their own questions. Lead them to conclude that the way to answer questions is through observation and research.
- Explain that scientists find answers to their questions in some of these same ways. Scientists will look at, or observe, things. They will also do research using books and the Internet.

Health

What Is It?

Objective: Use clues to answer questions.

Science Inquiry Skills: predict, interpret data, communicate

Materials
- crayons
- copies of What Is It? worksheet, page 124

Grouping whole group

Time 15 minutes

- Read children the three clues listed below. Ask them to identify the body part that answers the question.
  It is on my face.
  It is in the middle.
  It can smell things.
  What is it? (nose)
- Point out that children used the clues to answer the question, just as scientists use clues to answer questions.
- Challenge children to think of three clues about something related to health. Let them tell their clues to the group and see if the group can answer the What Is It? question.
- Distribute copies of the worksheet. Read aloud each set of clues to children. Have them color the picture that shows the answer to the question.

© Pearson Education, Inc. K

Math

How Many?

Objective: Subtract numbers to find answers.

Science Inquiry Skills:
observe, interpret data, communicate, record

Materials
- pencils

Grouping whole group

Time 15 minutes

- Have two children come to the front of the room. Give one child three pencils to hold. Ask the other child to take two of the pencils.
- Phrase the situation as a word problem: *[First child's name] had three pencils. [Second child's name] took two of the pencils. How many pencils does [first child's name] have now?* Children should answer that the first child has one pencil now.

- Use other situations with the pencils to model subtraction word problems. Each time ask children to answer the question.
- Write the following problem on the board: 3 – 2 = 1. Explain that the – sign stands for "take away" and the = sign stands for "equals": *3 take away 2 equals 1.*
- Continue with these problems: 6 – 1 = __, 4 – 3 = __. Remind children that the – sign means "take away." Have them draw pictures to show the problem and then write the answer on the line after the equals sign.

Social Studies

Where Is It?

Objective: Use a map to answer questions.

Science Inquiry Skills:
identify, observe, communicate

Materials
- blue, green, red crayons for each child
- copies of Where Is It? worksheet, page 125

Grouping whole group

Time 20 minutes

- Distribute the blue, green, and red crayons and copies of the worksheet. Explain that this is a map of a playground. The map shows what things are on the playground and where these things are located.
- Tell children that you will ask them questions about the playground. They will use the map and the crayons to answer the questions.

  Where are the swings? Encourage children to give the location. *Color the swings blue.*

  Where is the slide? Color the slide green.

  Does the playground have a sandbox? Where is it? Color it red.

  How many seesaws does the playground have? Draw a blue circle around the seesaws.

  Are the monkey bars closer to the swings or to the slide? Draw a green circle around the monkey bars.

© Pearson Education, Inc. K

Recycle, Reduce, Reuse

Use the worksheet on page 71 to introduce the letter R.

Science

Three Rs

Objective: Define recycle, reduce, and reuse and learn why it is important.

Science Inquiry Skills: identify, communicate, infer

Materials
- an empty milk carton
- the recycle symbol
- copies of Recycle or Not? worksheet, pages 126 and 127

Grouping whole group

Time 20 minutes

- Display an object with the recycle symbol. Tell children when they see this symbol on a large container, they should only place things in the container that can be recycled. Explain that *recycle* means to change something so that it can be used again. *Reduce* means to use less. *Reuse* means to use something again.
- Have children think of other ways that they or their families can recycle, reduce, or reuse. List their responses on the board.
- Distribute copies of the worksheet. Have them color and cut out the pictures. Have children glue the pictures from page 126 under the correct heading on page 127.

Art

Reuse a Milk Carton

Objective: Reuse materials in an arts and crafts activity.

Science Inquiry Skills: identify, infer, communicate, model

Materials
- small rocks
- potting soil
- flower seeds
- craft sticks
- empty milk cartons

Grouping individuals

Time 20 minutes

- Prior to lunch or snack time, tell children to place their empty milk cartons in a designated spot. Open the milk cartons up completely, then thoroughly rinse out the milk cartons.
- Tell children you are going to make a milk carton garden to make the classroom more beautiful. Place some small rocks in the bottom of the milk carton. Then fill the milk carton with potting soil. Next, place some seeds in the soil and cover them. Lastly, write your name and the type of flower seeds you planted on a craft stick. Place the craft stick in the milk carton planter.
- Have children water their plants and document the plant growth.

© Pearson Education, Inc. K

Reading

Reuse

Objective: Listen to a fictional story about reusing. Give examples of things that can be reused.

Science Inquiry Skills: identify, observe, interpret, communicate

Materials
- *Mike Mulligan and His Steam Shovel* by Virginia Lee Burton
- copies of Reuse It! worksheet, page 128
- crayons

Grouping whole group

Time 20 minutes

- Display the book *Mike Mulligan and His Steam Shovel.* Have children build oral vocabulary by asking them to name objects as you picture walk through the book.
- Read *Mike Mulligan and His Steam Shovel.* Ask children to retell the story.
- Open to pages 40 and 41 of *Mike Mulligan and His Steam Shovel.* Ask children how the townspeople in the story decided to *reuse* Mary Ann the steam shovel. Tell children that this probably wouldn't work in reality, but there are other things that we can reuse.
- Ask children to name things that can be reused, such as milk cartons, that can become flowerpots. List children's responses.
- Distribute the Reuse It! worksheet to children. Ask them to draw a picture of something they can reuse. Tell them to draw something named on the list or a different idea. Then have children write or dictate a sentence to describe their illustration. Collect the papers to create a class *Reuse It!* book.

Social Studies

Everyone Can Help

Objective: Recognize that it is everyone's responsibility to help protect Earth's land, water, and air.

Science Inquiry Skills: identify, communicate

Materials
- construction paper
- markers

Grouping small groups

Time 15 minutes one day, 30 minutes on another day

- Help children organize a school clean-up day. Prompt children to suggest ways they could help the entire school increase their awareness of recycling, reducing, and reusing.

- Guide children to think of slogans to promote *recycling, reducing,* and *reusing.* Write the suggestions on the board.

- Distribute construction paper and markers. Ask children to make signs reminding other students to recycle, reduce, and reuse. Help children post the signs throughout the school.
- Encourage children to become "model" recycling, reducing, and reusing citizens.

© Pearson Education, Inc. K

S

Spring, Summer, Fall, Winter

Use the worksheet on page 72 to introduce the letter S.

Science

Four Seasons

Objective: Read about the seasons.

Science Inquiry Skills: identify, observe, record

Materials
- *What Makes the Seasons?* by Megan Montague Cash (or another book about the seasons)
- pencils and crayons
- copies of Four Seasons worksheet, page 129

Grouping whole group

Time 20 minutes

- Read aloud the book about the seasons. Discuss the pictures with children. Have volunteers tell what activities they do in each season and which season they like best and why.
- Explain that spring, summer, fall, and winter are seasons, or times of year. Then give a clue about a season and have a volunteer name the season. Continue with other clues.
- Distribute copies of the worksheet. Have children cut out the names of the seasons and paste them under the appropriate pictures.

Science

Winter or Summer?

Objective: Compare and contrast two seasons.

Science Inquiry Skills: identify, classify, compare

Materials
- scissors
- paste
- copies of Winter or Summer? worksheet, page 130

Grouping whole group

Time 20 minutes

- Draw a flower on the board and write the word *summer* under the picture. Ask children to tell what they know about summer including clothing they might wear. Continue with a snowman for winter. Guide children as they compare and contrast the seasons.
- Distribute the worksheet and a piece of construction paper to each child. Read the words *Winter* and *Summer* to children. Have children name each picture and tell if it is something that you might see in the winter or the summer.
- Have children color the pictures, and then cut them out. Next have them fold their construction paper in half and glue the *Winter* label to the top of one side and *Summer* to the other side. Have children glue the pictures under the correct heading.

© Pearson Education, Inc. K

Music

What Season Is It?

Objective: Identify characteristics of seasons using a song.

Science Inquiry Skills:
identify, classify, communicate

Grouping whole group

Time 15 minutes

- Teach children the first verse of the song, "What Season Is It?" sung to the tune of "Here We Go 'Round the Mulberry Bush."
- After children sing the verse, have them answer the question: *What season is it when rain showers come and go? (spring)*
- Have children sing the verse for the other seasons, each time replacing the fourth line with one of the lines below. After singing each verse, have children identify the season they are singing about.

What Season Is It?
Do you know what season
it is,
Season it is, season it is?
Do you know what season
it is,
When rain showers come
and go?
Verse 2: When the Sun
shines very hot?
Verse 3: When the wind
blows leaves around?
Verse 4: When the snow
comes and stays?

Science

Spring Ducklings

Objective: Learn about the life cycle of a duck.

Science Inquiry Skills:
identify, communicate

Materials
- *Duckling Days* by Karen Wallace (or another book about the life cycle of a duck)
- crayons
- copies of Spring Ducklings worksheet, page 131

Grouping whole group

Time 15 minutes

- Tell children that many wild animals such as ducks have their babies in the spring.
- Read the book *Duckling Days*. After reading, picture walk through the book to lead a discussion on the life cycle of a duck.
- Distribute the copies of the worksheet. Tell children to color the pictures. Then have them number the pictures to show the life cycle of the duck.

© Pearson Education, Inc. K

Touch, See, Hear, Smell, Taste

Use the worksheet on page 73 to introduce the letter T.

Science

Our Five Senses

Objective: Understand what the five senses are and how people use them.

Science Inquiry Skills: identify, classify, infer

Materials
- bell
- crayons
- copies of Our Five Senses worksheet, page 132

Grouping whole group

Time 15 minutes

- Turn your back to children and ring the bell. Ask them what the object is *(bell)*, how they know that *(heard it ring)*, and what they used to hear the ringing. *(ears)*
- Describe the color and shape of an object in the room and have children identify it. Ask them what they used to see the object. *(eyes)*
- Tell children that we also use our noses to smell, our mouths to taste, and our hands to touch. These are called the *five senses*.
- Distribute the copies of the worksheet. Have children draw a line to match each object with the sense they would most likely use to find out about the object. Review their answers.

Social Studies

Senses for Safety

Objective: Recognize that the senses can help keep people safe.

Science Inquiry Skills: identify, observe, communicate

Materials
- crayons
- copies of Senses for Safety worksheet, page 133

Grouping whole group

Time 15 minutes

- Ask children what they should do before they begin to cross a street. *(stop, look both ways, listen)* Have several volunteers demonstrate these actions. Ask children what senses the actors used when they stopped, looked both ways, and listened. Help children conclude that seeing and hearing can help keep them safe.

- Have other volunteers act out additional situations in which the senses help us, such as hearing a fire engine's siren, seeing a tornado, or smelling the smoke from a fire.
- Distribute copies of the worksheet. Ask children to talk about which senses they would most likely use when they get off the school bus and when they cross the street. Have children color the worksheet.

© Pearson Education, Inc. K

Reading

Using My Senses

Objective: Read about how a child uses his senses.

Science Inquiry Skills: identify, observe, communicate

Materials
- *My Five Senses* by Aliki (or another book about the senses)
- crayons
- copies of the Using My Senses worksheet, page 134

Grouping whole group

Time 20 minutes

- Read aloud the book *My Five Senses* by Aliki. Discuss the pictures with children. Turn to page 3, read each column heading, and have volunteers identify the objects in the column.
- Distribute copies of the worksheet. Explain to children that the small pictures stand for the five senses. Have children draw a picture of something they would identify by using a specific sense. For example, they might draw a jet plane next to the ear.

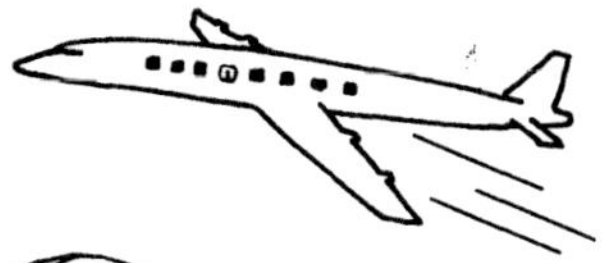

- Encourage children to show and explain their pictures.

Music

The Senses Song

Objective: Sing a song about the senses.

Science Inquiry Skills: identify, communicate

Grouping whole group

Time 15 minutes

- Sing the question verse of the song "The Senses Song" to the tune of "Mary Had a Little Lamb." Name an object you can see, such as the Sun.
- Teach children the answer verse of the song. Have them repeat the object you named.
- Sing the question verse four more times, substituting *hear, smell, taste,* and *touch* for *see* and naming appropriate objects.
- Each time have children respond with the answer verse, using the same sense word and object name.

The Senses Song

Question verse
Do you see what I can see,
I can see, I can see?
Do you see what I can see?
I can see ___. (the Sun)

Answer verse
I can see what you can see,
You can see, you can see.
I can see what you can see.
I can see the Sun.

Verse 2: . . . hear . . . rain.
Verse 3: . . . smell . . . popcorn.
Verse 4: . . . taste . . . cherries.
Verse 5: . . . touch . . . my cat.

© Pearson Education, Inc. K

Up, Up, Up into Space

Use the worksheet on page 74 to introduce the letter U.

Science

The Planets

Objective: Identify and name the planets of the solar system.

Science Inquiry Skills: identify, model, communicate

Materials
- *Spinning in Space: A Book About the Planets* by Dana Meachen Rau (or another book about the planets)
- crayons
- 6" x 18" pieces of construction paper for each child
- copies of The Planets worksheet, page 135

Grouping whole group

Time 20 minutes

- Display a globe. Remind children that the globe is a model of the Earth. Tell them that we live on the planet called Earth. Ask children to name other planets in our solar system.
- Read *Spinning in Space.* After reading, ask children to recall facts that they learned about each planet. Tell children that it has recently been decided that Pluto is no longer a planet.
- Draw eight circles on the board. Ask children to help you name each planet in the order it appears in the solar system.
- Distribute copies of the worksheet, page 135. Have children color each planet and cut the planets out. Then have them glue each planet in order on a piece of construction paper.

Writing

Astronauts

Objective: Learn about the job of an astronaut.

Science Inquiry Skills: communicate, classify, describe

Materials
- *Rockets and Spaceships* by Karen Wallace (or another book about astronauts)
- copies of Astronauts worksheet, page 136

Grouping whole group

Time 20 minutes

- Draw a *KWL* chart on the board. Ask children what they know about astronauts. Write their responses under the *K* portion of the chart. Then ask children what they want to learn about astronauts. Write the responses under the *W* portion of the chart.
- Read *Rockets and Spaceships*. After reading, ask children what they learned about astronauts. List their responses under the *L* portion of the chart.
- Distribute copies of the worksheet. Have children color the astronaut outline to look like themselves. Then have them cut out the astronaut.

© Pearson Education, Inc. K

Science

The Sun Is a Star

Objective: Learn about the Sun.

Science Inquiry Skills: identify, observe, classify, communicate

Materials
- *The Sun* by Ralph Winrich (or another nonfiction text about the Sun)
- a large piece of yellow butcher paper

Grouping whole group

Time 15 minutes

- Cut out a very large, yellow circle in the shape of the Sun. Near the top of the circle, write *Sun Facts.* Then attach the Sun to chart paper.
- Read *The Sun.*
- Ask children to recall facts about the Sun. List their responses on the large Sun cutout.

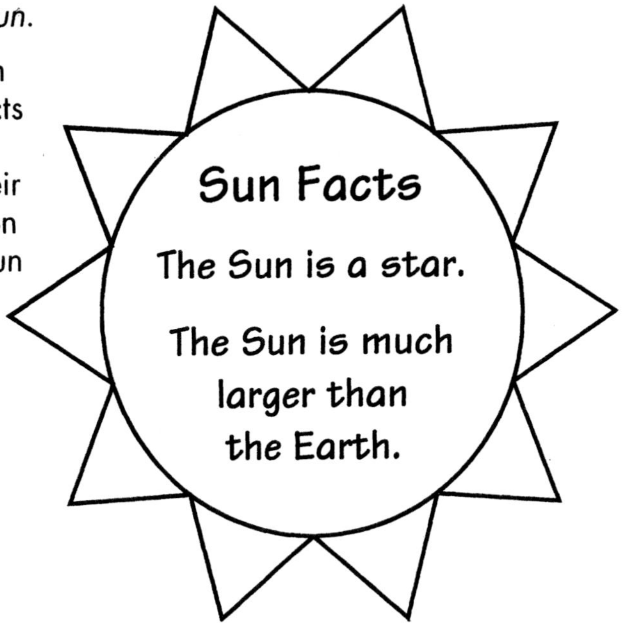

Music

Five Little Astronauts

Objective: Learn a finger play about astronauts.

Science Inquiry Skills: communicate

Grouping whole group

Time 10 minutes

- Teach children the following finger play.

Five Little Astronauts

Five little astronauts in their spacesuits snug.
The first one said, "Oh my, it's getting late."
The second one said, "We'd better close the gate."
The third one said, "We are going to zip all around."
The fourth one said, "We aren't on the ground."
The fifth one said, "Oh look, we're in space."
The five little astronauts flew 'round and 'round at a tremendous pace.

© Pearson Education, Inc. K

Valleys, Plains, Mountains

Use the worksheet on page 75 to introduce the letter V.

Science

Kinds of Land

Objective: Identify three kinds of landforms on Earth.

Science Inquiry Skills: identify, observe, make a model

Materials
- modeling clay
- crayons
- copies of Kinds of Land worksheet, page 137

Grouping small groups

Time 20 minutes

- Tell children the Earth is made of many types of landforms. Three of the landforms are called *valleys, plains,* and *mountains.*
- On the board, draw two mountains. Point to the mountains and tell children that these are called *mountains.* Point to the area between the mountains and tell children this is a *valley.* Draw an area of flat grasslands and tell children that this type of landform is called the *plains.*
- Divide children into small groups. Give each group some modeling clay. Have the groups use the modeling clay to make the three kinds of landforms.
- Distribute copies of the worksheet. Ask children to cut out and paste each landform name under the correct picture. Together check children's answers.

Science

Animals of the Plains

Objective: Identify animals that live on the plains.

Science Inquiry Skills: identify, observe, compare, communicate

Materials
- *Animal Babies in Grasslands* by Jennifer Schofield
- crayons
- copies of Animals of the Plains worksheet, page 138

Grouping whole group

Time 20 minutes

- Tell children that almost one-fourth of the Earth's land is plains. There are many different words used to describe this type of landform—plains, grasslands, savannas, and prairies.
- Read *Animal Babies in Grasslands.*
- Ask children to name some of the animals found living in plains, or grasslands, around the world.
- Distribute copies of the Animals of the Plains worksheet. Have children color the animals and the background. Then have them cut out the animals and glue them into the plains scene.

© Pearson Education, Inc. K

Music

Valley Low, Mountain High

Objective: Sing about three kinds of land.

Science Inquiry Skills: identify, communicate

Grouping whole group

Time 15 minutes

- Teach children the song "Down in the Valley."
- For the first verse, show children how to put their arms together down in front of them to show the valley. For the second verse, have them put their arms together high over their heads to show the mountain.
- Help children write lyrics for a third verse about plains and sing it together. Have them fold their arms and lay one on top of the other in front of them to show the flat plains.

Down in the Valley

Down in the valley,
Valley so low,
Hang your head over.
Hear the wind blow.
Hear the wind blow,
dear.
Hear the wind blow,
Down in the valley,
Valley so low.

Up on the mountain,
Mountain so high,
Hang your head over.
Hear the wind cry.
Hear the wind cry, dear.
Hear the wind cry,
Up on the mountain,
Mountain so high.

Reading

Bear Hunt

Objective: Learn about an animal of the plains.

Science Inquiry Skills: identify, model, communicate

Materials
- *We're Going on a Bear Hunt* by Michael Rosen

Grouping whole group

Time 20 minutes

- Remind children that the plains or grasslands are usually covered with tall grasses that can survive in hot, dry summers.
- Tell children that you are going to read a book whose story takes place in different kinds of water and land, including the plains.
- Read *We're Going on a Bear Hunt* several times. Encourage children to join in.

© Pearson Education, Inc. K

Weather

Use the worksheet on page 76 to introduce the letter W.

Science — Weather Watch

Objective: Describe the weather each day.

Science Inquiry Skills: observe, identify, collect data, record

Materials
- class weather chart
- crayons or markers
- copies of Weather Watch worksheet, page 139

Grouping whole group

Time 10 minutes each day for five days

- Draw small pictures of a Sun, raindrops, clouds, a kite, and snowflakes. Tell children the Sun stands for *sunny*, the raindrops for *rainy*, the clouds for *cloudy*, the kite for *windy*, and the snowflakes for *snowy*.
- Ask children to describe today's weather using one of these words: *sunny, rainy, cloudy, windy, snowy*.
- Distribute copies of the worksheet. Have children draw the weather symbol in the appropriate space.
- Repeat this activity every day for five days until children have completed their weather charts.

Music — What's the Weather Like?

Objective: Tell about the weather in a song.

Science Inquiry Skills: observe, identify, communicate

Grouping whole group

Time 15 minutes

- Ask children what the weather is like in the spring. Prompt with questions if necessary: *Is it rainy? Is it warm? Is it windy?*
- Teach children the "What's the Weather Like?" song, sung to the tune of "Mary Had a Little Lamb." In the second verse, use the adjectives children offered when they described spring weather.
- Have children describe the weather in the summer, fall, and winter. Sing the song three more times, changing the name of the season and the adjectives each time.

What's the Weather Like?

Tell me what's the weather like,
The weather like, the weather like.
Tell me what's the weather like,
The weather in the spring.

In the spring it's rainy and warm,
Rainy and warm, rainy and warm,
In the spring it's rainy and warm.
The weather is rainy and warm.

© Pearson Education, Inc. K

Reading/Art

We Know Weather

Objective: Read about different kinds of weather and draw a picture of one kind.

Science Inquiry Skills: identify, observe, communicate

Materials
- *Whatever the Weather* by Karen Wallace or *What's the Weather Today?* by Allan Fowler (or another book about kinds of weather)
- crayons
- sheets of drawing paper

Grouping whole group

Time 20 minutes

- Read aloud the book about weather. Discuss the pictures with children. As you point to a picture showing one kind of weather, have volunteers tell about their experiences with that kind of weather.
- Ask children what their favorite kind of weather is and why. Have them draw a picture of themselves enjoying that weather.
- Display the pictures on a bulletin board, grouping those that show the same kind of weather.

Writing

The Weather Report

Objective: Complete a sentence about the weather.

Science Inquiry Skills: identify, communicate

Materials
- pencils and crayons
- copies of The Weather Report worksheet, page 140

Grouping whole group

Time 15 minutes

- Discuss words children have used to describe the weather, such as *sunny, rainy, cloudy, windy,* and *snowy.* Ask them which of these words tells what today's weather is like.
- Distribute copies of the worksheet. Read aloud the sentence frame. Have children complete the sentence by writing the word they used to describe the weather today. Ask them to draw a picture in the box to go with their sentence.
- Have children share their sentences and pictures.

The Weather Report

Today is Sunny.

sunny rainy cloudy windy snowy

© Pearson Education, Inc. K

X-tra Special X rays

Use the worksheet on page 77 to introduce the letter X.

Science/Reading X-tra Special X rays

Objective: Learn about X rays.

Science Inquiry Skills: identify, observe, infer, communicate

Materials
- *Bones* by Stephen Krensky
- crayons
- glue
- cotton swabs
- copies of X-tra Special X rays worksheet, page 141

Grouping whole group

Time 20 minutes

- Display the cover of the book. Ask children to describe the cover illustration. Point to the X ray. Tell children an X ray is a picture of your bones.
- Read aloud the book *Bones* by Stephen Krensky.
- Picture walk through the book again and ask children to recall facts about bones. List their responses on the board.
- Distribute copies of the X-tra Special X rays worksheet and cotton swabs to children. Ask children to glue cotton swabs in the outline of a child to represent bones in their body. Then have them color the face to look like themselves.

Music Do You Know What an X ray Is?

Objective: Learn a song about X rays.

Science Inquiry Skills: identify, communicate

Grouping whole group

Time 10 minutes

- Remind children that we can't see our bones. Ask them to recall what a doctor does when she needs to look at someone's bones. *(take an x ray)*
- Teach children the song "Do You Know What an X ray Is?" sung to the tune of "Do You Know the Muffin Man?"

Do You Know What an X ray Is?

Oh, do you know what
an X ray is?
An X ray is? An X ray is?
Oh, do you know what
an X ray is?
It's a snapshot of your
bones!

- Have children sing the song several times.

© Pearson Education, Inc. K

Math

Bone Patterns

Objective: Create a pattern.

Science Inquiry Skills:
observe, interpret data, communicate, compare

Materials
- twenty construction paper bones in each of the following colors—red, blue, and yellow
- 6" x 18" white construction paper strips for each small group of children
- glue

Grouping small groups

Time 20 minutes

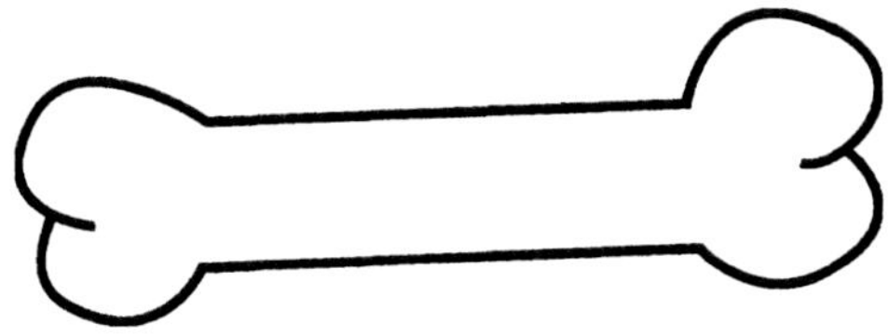

- Prior to the lesson, cut out 20 construction paper bones in each of the following colors: red, blue, and yellow. Divide the bones into five small groups. Each small group should have four red, four blue, and four yellow construction paper bones.
- Remind children that bones help people and animals stand, walk, run, and hop. Ask children to recall other facts about bones.
- Divide children into five small groups. Give each group a set of construction paper bones and a white strip of construction paper.
- Ask each group to make a bone color pattern. When they have finished the pattern, ask them to glue it to the strip of white paper.
- When each group has finished, display the patterns on a bulletin board. Ask children to compare and contrast the pattern each group created.

Writing

My Bones

Objective: Write about bones.

Science Inquiry Skills:
identify, communicate

Materials
- copies of the My Bones worksheet, page 142
- scissors
- crayons

Grouping whole group

Time 15 minutes

- Tell children that they are going to make a book about bones.
- Distribute copies of the My Bones worksheet, page 142. Read each section with children. Help them fill in the missing number or word.
- Have children color the pictures in their book and cut the pages apart. Ask children to put the pages in order. Then staple the pages together to make a book.

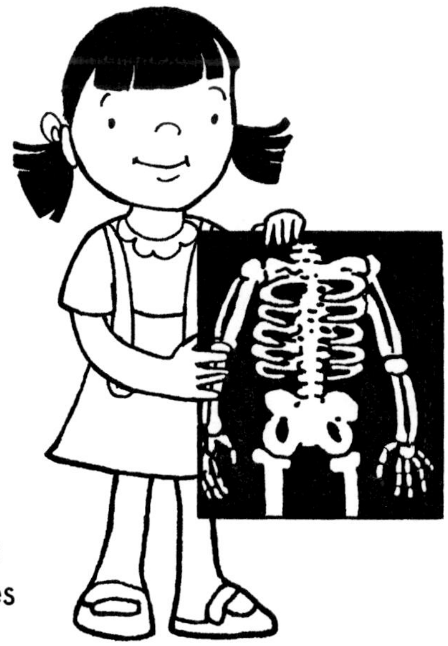

© Pearson Education, Inc. K

Your Shadow

Use the worksheet on page 78 to introduce the letter Y.

Science

Making Shadows

Objective: Discover how shadows are made.

Science Inquiry Skills: observe, identify, communicate

Materials
- flashlight
- crayons or markers
- copies of Making Shadows worksheet, page 143

Grouping whole group

Time 20 minutes

- Have a volunteer shine the flashlight on one hand to make a shadow on the wall. Ask children to tell what they see on the wall. *(shadow)*
- Let children take turns making shadows with classroom objects such as a book, a pencil, a ruler, and a stuffed toy. Ask children why these objects have shadows. *(They are solid; they block out the light.)*
- Distribute copies of the Making Shadows worksheet. Point out that the Sun at the top of the page is shining down on the square, circle, and rectangle. Ask children to draw the shadow that each shape will make on the ground below.

Reading

Sun and Shadow

Objective: Read a poem about the relationship between the Sun and shadows.

Science Inquiry Skills: observe, identify, communicate

Materials
- flashlight

Grouping whole group

Time 15 minutes

- Write the poem "Sun and Shadow" on the board and read it aloud to children several times.
- Choose one child to be the "Sun" and give that child the flashlight. Choose another child to be the narrator of the poem. Have the pair make the narrator's shadow appear and disappear as the group reads the poem aloud together.
- Ask a volunteer to find the words *Sun* and *shadow* in the poem. Have the child circle the words on the board. Point out that these words are in the poem more than once.

Sun and Shadow

When the Sun is
  shining brightly,
I see my shadow,
  clear as day.
But watch my
  shadow disappear
When clouds make
  the Sun go away.

© Pearson Education, Inc. K

Science

What Has a Shadow?

Objective: Identify objects that can make shadows.

Science Inquiry Skills: identify, observe, communicate

Materials
- flashlight, one for each group
- sheet of wax paper, clear plastic sandwich bag, sheet of cardboard, piece of heavy fabric, wood block, small aluminum pan
- crayons or markers
- copies of What Has a Shadow? worksheet, page 144

Grouping small groups

Time 20 minutes

- Divide children into six groups. Give each group a flashlight and one of the six objects. Have the groups hold their object in front of a wall, shine the flashlight on the object, and see whether the object makes a shadow.
- Have each group tell whether its object had a shadow or not.
- Distribute copies of the What Has a Shadow? worksheet. Have children circle the objects that can make shadows. Ask them to explain their answers.

Music

Shadow Dancing

Objective: Move the way that the shadows do.

Science Inquiry Skills: observe, identify

Materials
- music with a strong beat
- flashlight

Grouping whole group

Time 15 minutes

- Ask a volunteer to stand in front of a wall and face the group. Whisper an action, such as hop, spin, twist, sway, or bend, to the child.
- Play the music and have the child demonstrate the action in time to the beat. Shine the flashlight on the child to make a shadow on the wall.
- Ask the other children to watch the "dancing" shadow and identify what action it is doing.
- Have all children perform the action in time to the music.
- Continue with other volunteer dancers and other actions.

© Pearson Education, Inc. K

Z Zoos

Use the worksheet on page 79 to introduce the letter Z.

Science/Reading Who's at a Zoo?

Objective: Recognize that zoos provide homes for many wild animals.

Science Inquiry Skills: identify, communicate

Materials
- *A Visit to the Zoo* by B. A. Hoena or *Animals in the Zoo* by Allan Fowler or another book about zoos and zoo animals
- crayons
- copies of Who's at a Zoo? worksheet, page 145

Grouping whole group

Time 20 minutes

- Ask children to share their experiences visiting zoos, including what animals they saw and what the animals' zoo homes looked like.

- Read aloud the book about zoos. Discuss the pictures with children. Ask them to describe the zoo animals and tell what they know about each animal and its home.

- Distribute copies of the Who's at a Zoo? worksheet. Have children color the wild animals that they might see at a zoo.

Art Do a Zoo

Objective: Draw animals and their homes in a zoo.

Science Inquiry Skills: identify, communicate

Materials
- large sheets of drawing paper
- crayons
- animal books

Grouping small groups

Time 20 minutes

- Divide children into groups of three. Give each group a sheet of drawing paper, crayons, and a kind of zoo animal, such as elephants, tigers, lions, monkeys, giraffes, or zebras.

- Ask the groups to draw pictures of their animals in their homes in a zoo. Encourage children to look in the animal books if they need information for their pictures.
- Post the finished pictures around the room to make a zoo. Take a zoo tour by having each group tell about its animals. Save the pictures for the "Zoo Animal Count" activity.

© Pearson Education, Inc. K

Math

Zoo Animal Count

Objective: Count animals and write numbers.

Science Inquiry Skills: identify, observe, communicate

Materials
- pictures from the "Do a Zoo" activity or other pictures that show more than one zoo animal
- crayons
- copies of Zoo Animal Count worksheet, page 146

Grouping whole group

Time 20 minutes

- Show children one of the pictures from the "Do a Zoo" activity. Ask them how many animals they see. Write the number on the board.
- Continue with other pictures. Show two or more pictures together to get different and larger numbers. Or show several pictures and ask children to count all the brown animals, all the big animals, or all the animals with four legs.
- Distribute copies of the Zoo Animal Count worksheet. Have children count each set of animals and write the number. Check their answers.

Art

No Two Are Alike

Objective: Discuss unique qualities of zebras and human fingerprints.

Science Inquiry Skills: identify, communicate, compare

Materials
- photographs of zebras
- large index cards
- inkpad

Grouping whole group

Time 20 minutes

- Display pictures of zebras. Ask children to describe and name the animal. Tell them that zebras live in Africa and in zoos.
- Remind children that all zebras are black and white. Zebras are unique because no two zebras have exactly the same stripes.
- Ask children what people have in common with zebras. Lead them to determine that no two people are exactly alike.
- Tell children that fingerprints are unique to each person. Fingerprints are often used for identification. Even when they were first born, the nurse made a copy of their fingerprints.
- Give each child a large index card. Ask them to write their name on the card. Have children press their thumb on the inkpad, then on their index card. Encourage children to compare and contrast their thumbprints.

© Pearson Education, Inc. K

A is for

alligator

ant

apple

astronaut

© Pearson Education, Inc. K

B is for

battery

bear

bicycle

bird

© Pearson Education, Inc. K

C is for

cat

cloud

computer

cactus

© Pearson Education, Inc. K

D is for

desert

dolphin

drum

dog

© Pearson Education, Inc. K

E is for

electricity

eggs

Earth

elephant

© Pearson Education, Inc. K

F is for

flower

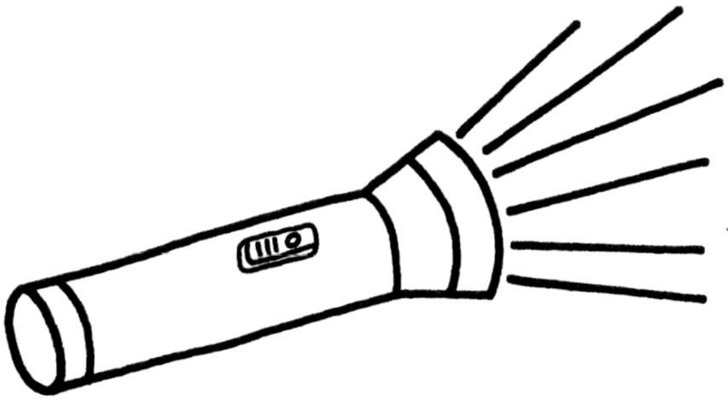

flashlight

fish

fire

© Pearson Education, Inc. K

G is for

goose

garden

glass

girl

© Pearson Education, Inc. K

H is for

hill

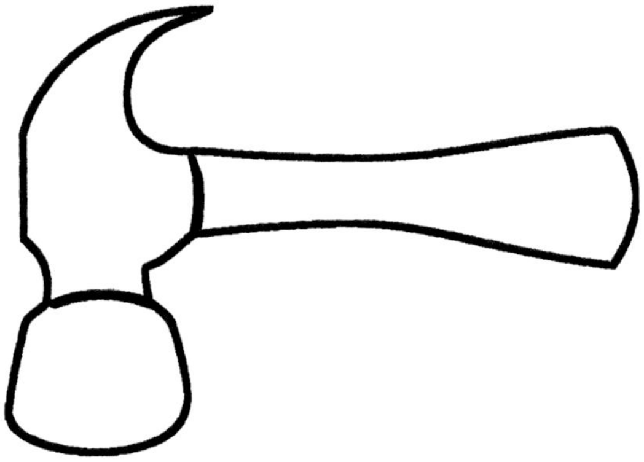

hammer

hen

horse

© Pearson Education, Inc. K

I is for

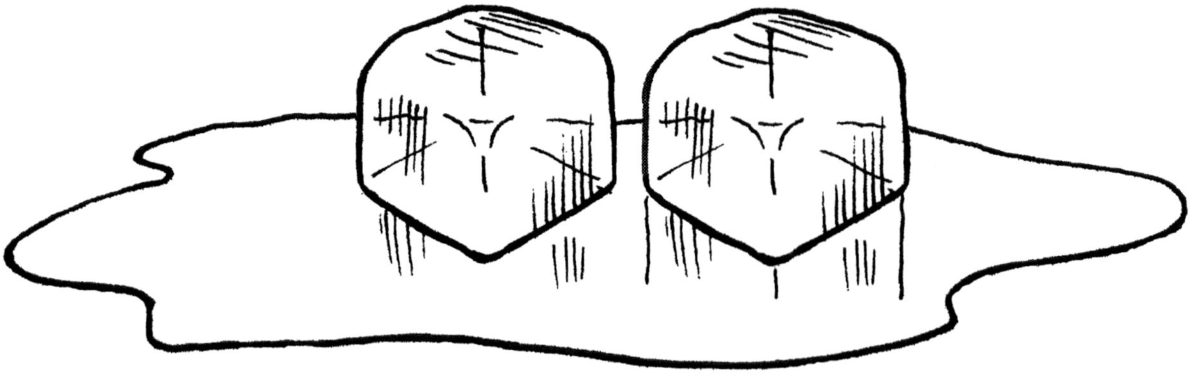

ice

insect

© Pearson Education, Inc. K

J is for

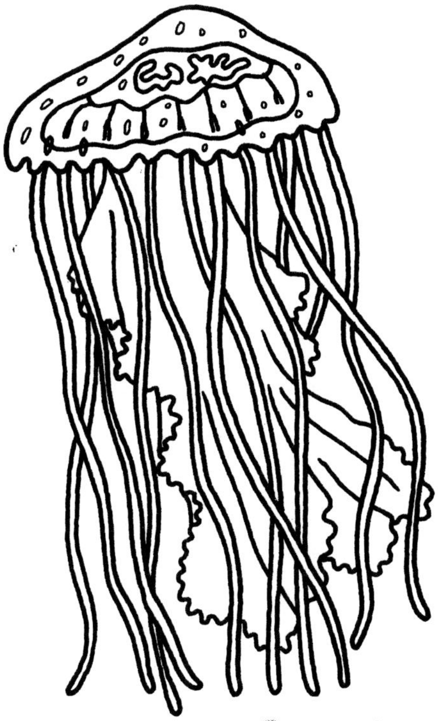

jellyfish

Jupiter

jet

© Pearson Education, Inc. K

K is for

kangaroo

key

kitten

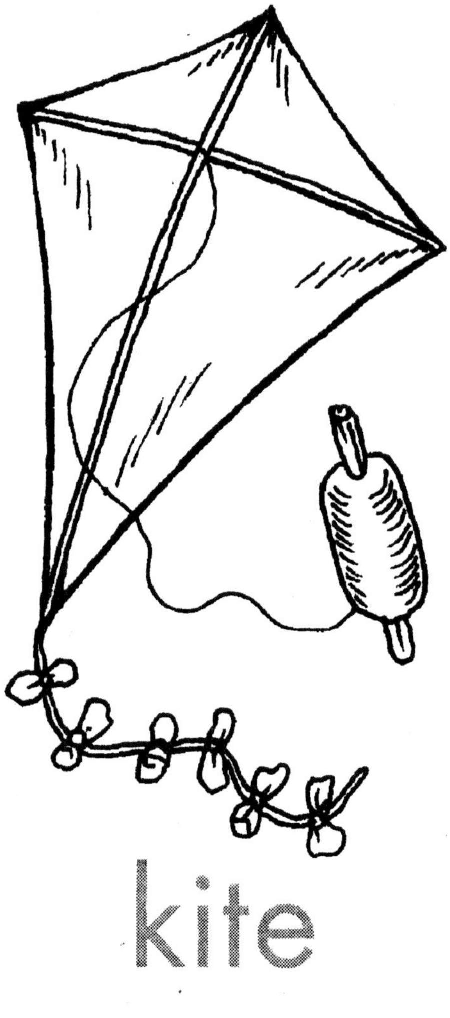

kite

© Pearson Education, Inc. K

L is for

land

lizard

lightning

leaf

© Pearson Education, Inc. K

M is for

move

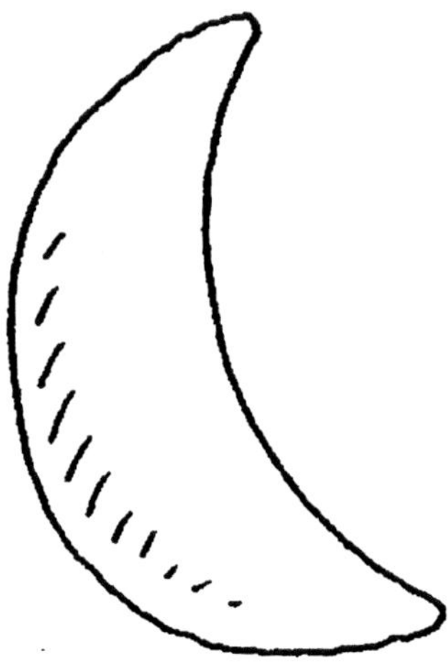

Moon

mountain

© Pearson Education, Inc. K

N is for

nose

nest

night

© Pearson Education, Inc. K

O is for

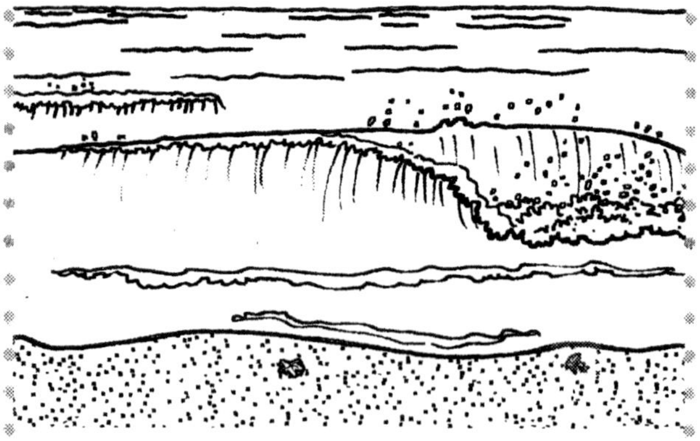

ocean

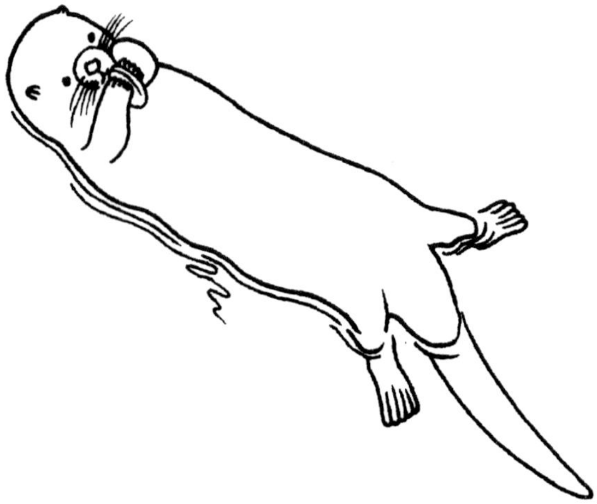

otter

ox

octopus

© Pearson Education, Inc. K

P is for

plug

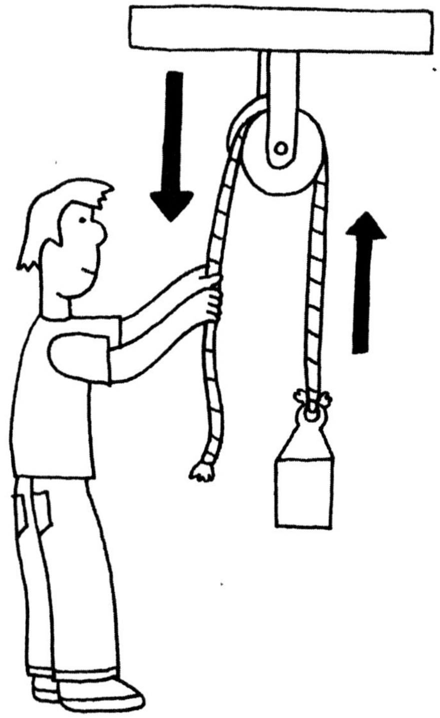

pulley

pond

© Pearson Education, Inc. K

Q is for

quail

quart

© Pearson Education, Inc. K

R is for

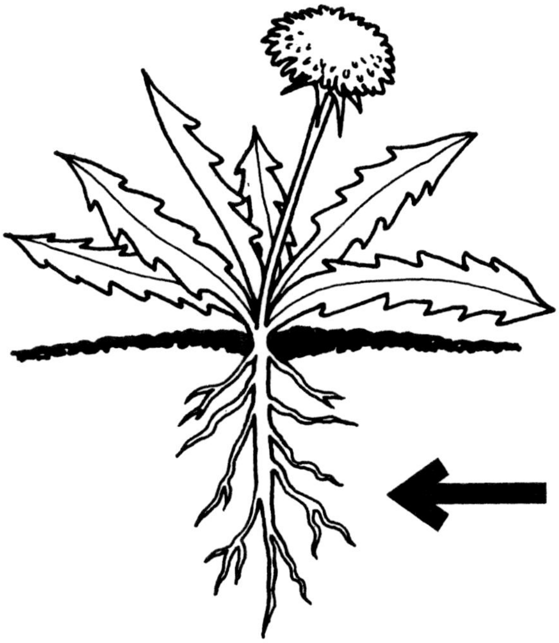

roots

rock

rainy

river

© Pearson Education, Inc. K

S is for

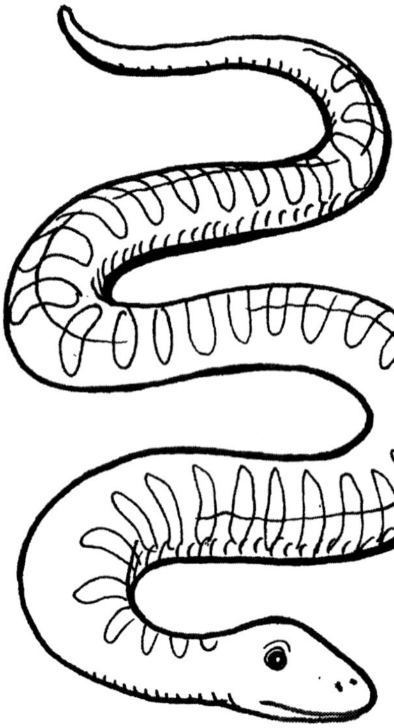

snake

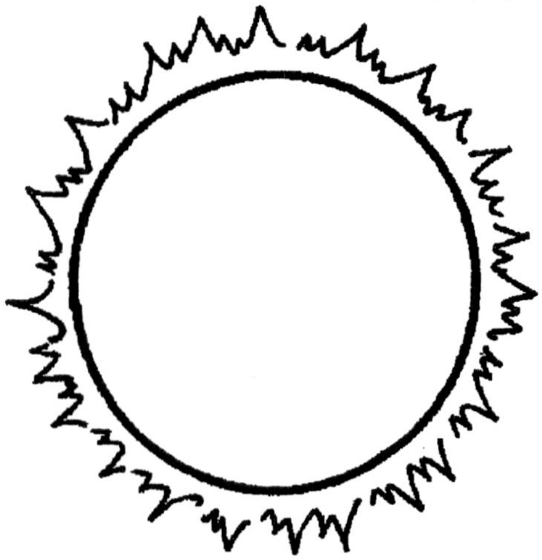

Sun

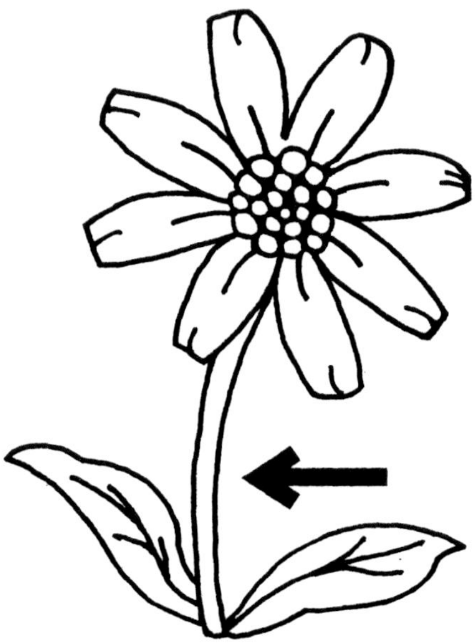

stem

shadow

© Pearson Education, Inc. K

T is for

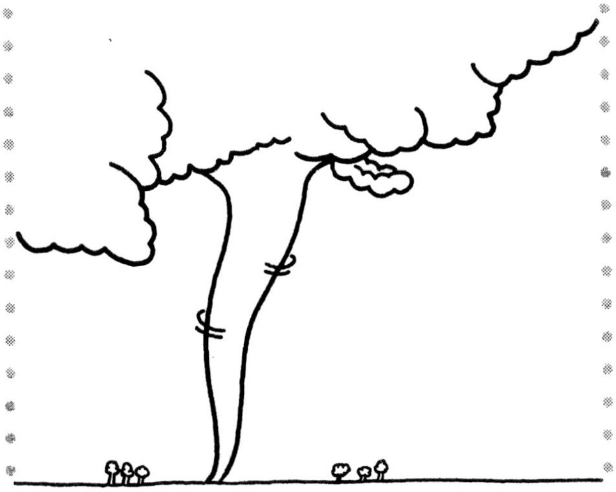

tornado

turkey

tree

tail

© Pearson Education, Inc. K

U is for

umbrella

under

© Pearson Education, Inc. K

V is for

vase

vacuum

volcano

vegetables

© Pearson Education, Inc. K

W is for

windy

water

wheel

wolf

© Pearson Education, Inc. K

X is for

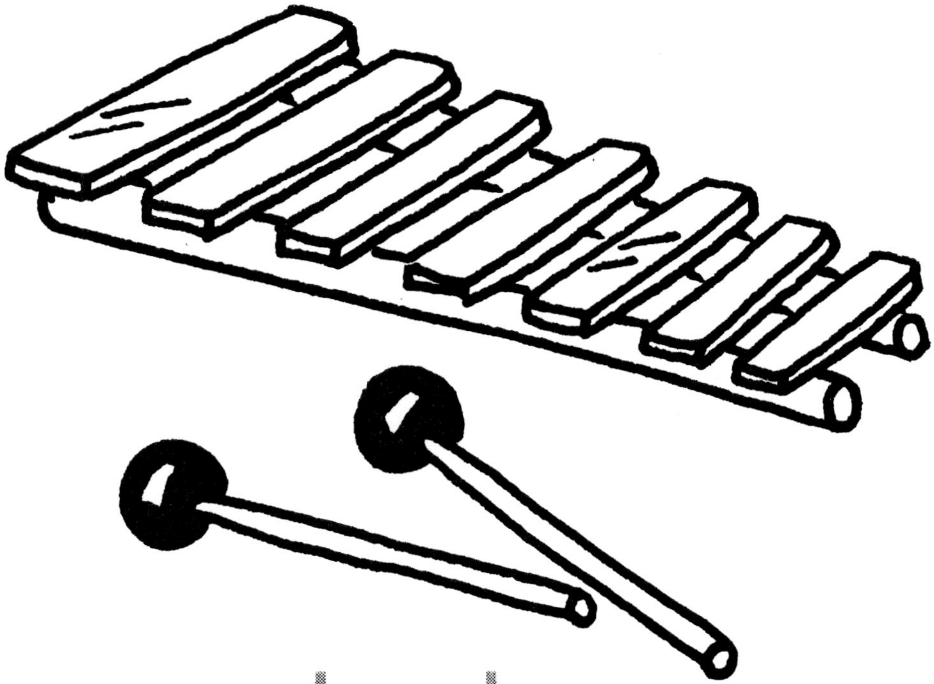

xylophone

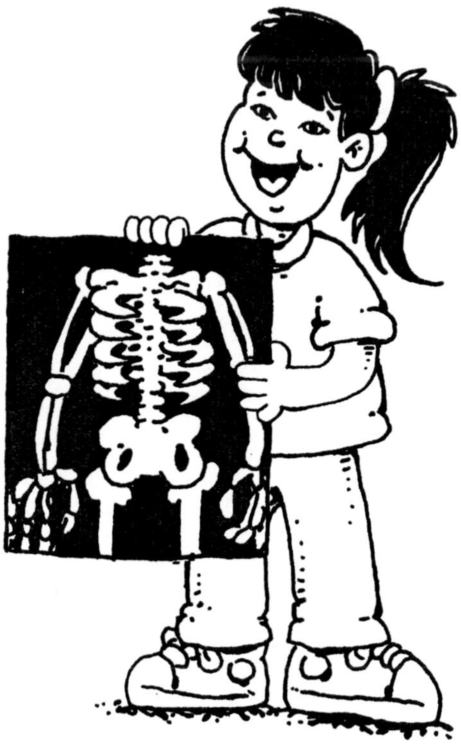

X-ray

© Pearson Education, Inc. K

Y is for

young

yak

yarn

yo-yo

© Pearson Education, Inc. K

Z is for

zebra

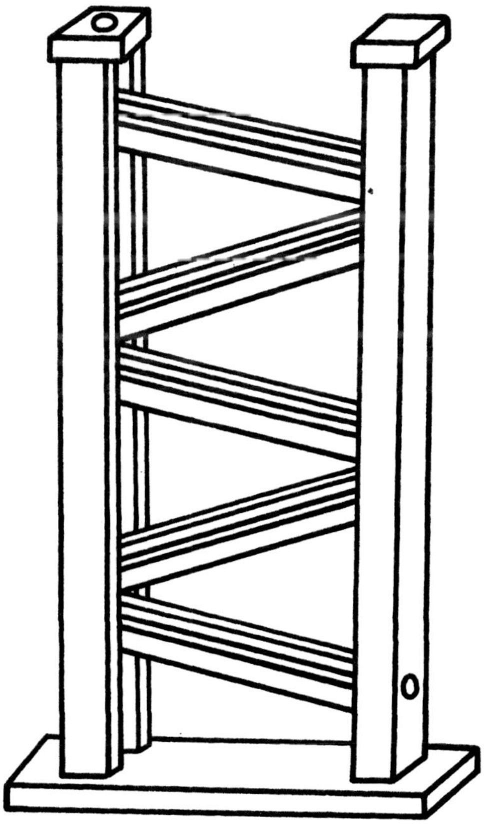

zigzag

zipper

© Pearson Education, Inc. K

Name ______________________

What Animals Need

Animal	Water	Food	Shelter
dog			

© Pearson Education, Inc. K

Name ______________________

My Favorite Animal

This is a ______________________.

© Pearson Education, Inc. K

Name ______________________

Animals Around the World

rain forest

grassland

desert

tundra

ocean

forest

© Pearson Education, Inc. K

Name

Name That Body Part

© Pearson Education, Inc. K

Name

A Healthy Body

1. Get Exercise

2. Eat Right

3. Keep Clean

© Pearson Education, Inc. K

Name ______________________________

Tell About Me

I ______________________________.

© Pearson Education, Inc. K

Name

A Butterfly's Life

© Pearson Education, Inc. K

Name ____________________

Change and Grow

Then

Then I ____________________.

Now

Now I ____________________.

© Pearson Education, Inc. K

Name

Little to Big

© Pearson Education, Inc. K

Name

Day to Night, Night to Day

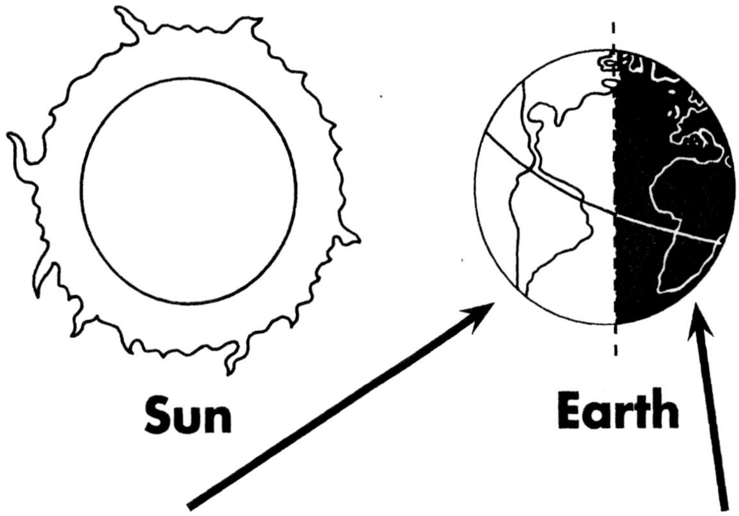

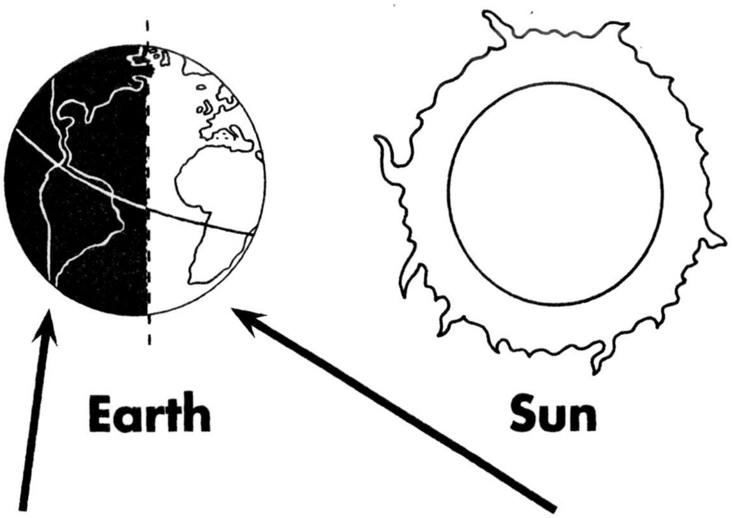

© Pearson Education, Inc. K

Name

Day or Night?

Sun | Moon | clouds
dark | stars | light

© Pearson Education, Inc. K

Name ______________________

Day Sky, Night Sky

In the day sky

I see ______________________.

In the night sky

I see ______________________.

© Pearson Education, Inc. K

Name

Wonderful, Marvelous Dirt!

© Pearson Education, Inc. K

Name ______________________

Earthworms

The Story of

______________________'s

Worm

This is my worm.
Its name is

______________________.

My worm likes to

____

on rainy days.

My worm helps flowers
and plants to grow.

© Pearson Education, Inc. K

Name ______________________

Earth Rocks!

© Pearson Education, Inc. K

Name ______________________

Is It Fast or Slow?

Fast	Slow

© Pearson Education, Inc. K

Name ______________________

Is It Loud or Soft?

Loud	Soft

© Pearson Education, Inc. K

Name ____________________

Which Is Faster?

© Pearson Education, Inc. K

Name ____________________

What Is It?

Gas	Liquid	Solid

© Pearson Education, Inc. K

Name ______________________

Watch the Changes!

From Liquid (water)	→	To Solid (ice)
From Solid (ice)	**→**	**To Liquid (water)**
From Liquid (water)	**→**	**To Gas (water vapor)**

© Pearson Education, Inc. K

Name ______________________

All Steamed Up

liquid

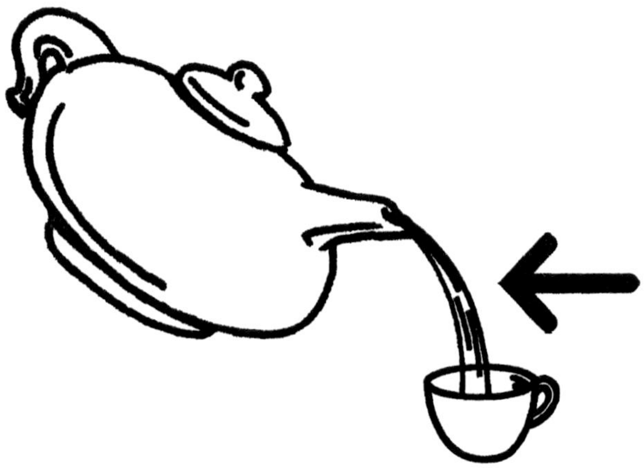

gas

solid

© Pearson Education, Inc. K

Name

Heat and Light

Heat
Light

© Pearson Education, Inc. K

Name

The Sun

The Sun is...

© Pearson Education, Inc. K

Name ______________________

Write a Rhyme

Where is the heat?

It is by my ______________________.

Look at the light.

It is so ______________________!

© Pearson Education, Inc. K

Name

How Should I Travel?

© Pearson Education, Inc. K

Name

Here Comes the Mail!

Dear ,

Love,

© Pearson Education, Inc. K

Name ____________________

Ways to Move

She jumps. She runs.

He hops. He walks.

She skips. She twirls.

He marches. He slides.

© Pearson Education, Inc. K

Name

Action Words

© Pearson Education, Inc. K

Name ______________________________

Where Is My Home?

© Pearson Education, Inc. K

Name

Over in the Meadow

five bees

Over in the Meadow

Name ___________

seven frogs

three owls

two fish

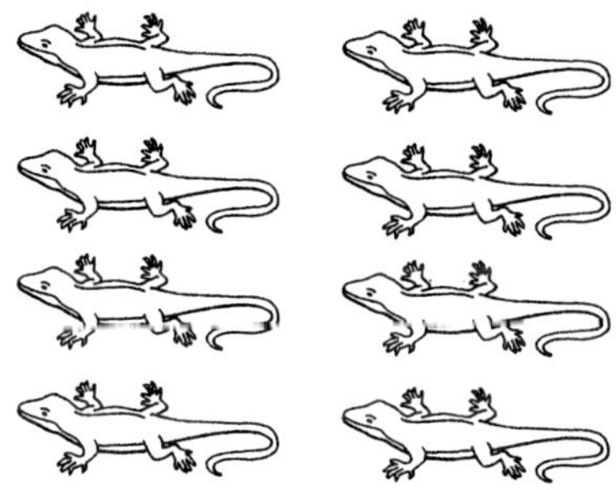

eight lizards

ten beavers

four rats

nine ducks

one turtle

six crows

© Pearson Education, Inc. K

Name ______________________

Finger Puppets

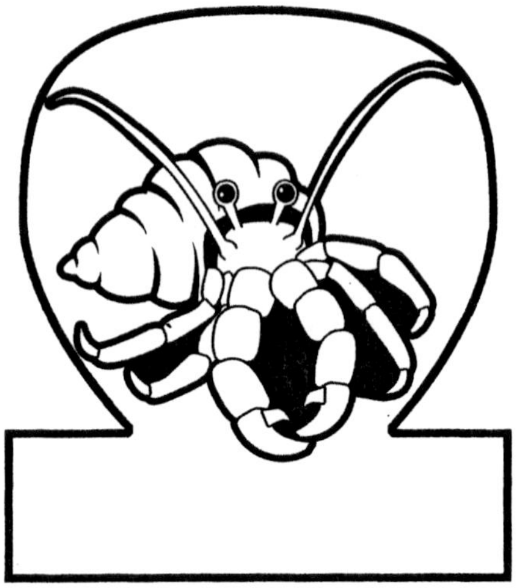

© Pearson Education, Inc. K

Name ______________________

Simple Machines

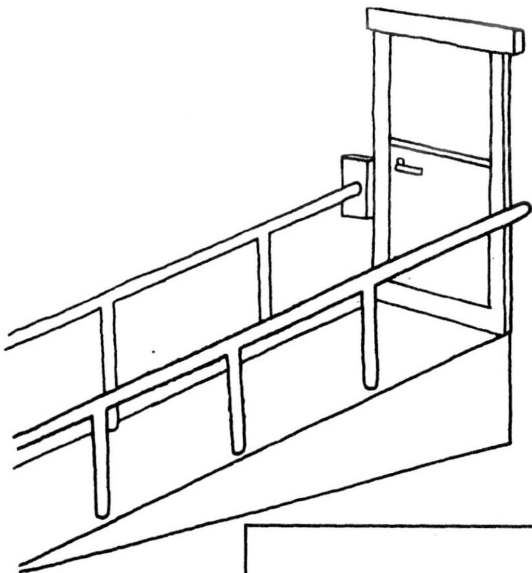

wheel	pulley	ramp	lever

© Pearson Education, Inc. K

Name

Wheel Count

© Pearson Education, Inc. K

Name

Finish the Words

1. goes 'round and 'round
2. looks like a long stick
3. always at a tilt
4. needs a rope, a string, or a chain

© Pearson Education, Inc. K

Name

Magnetic Math

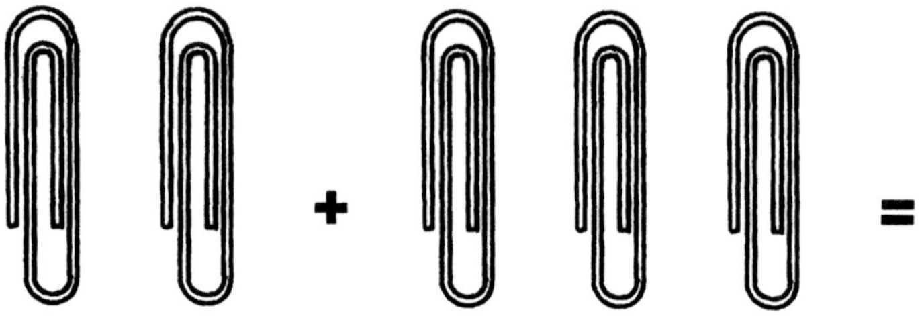

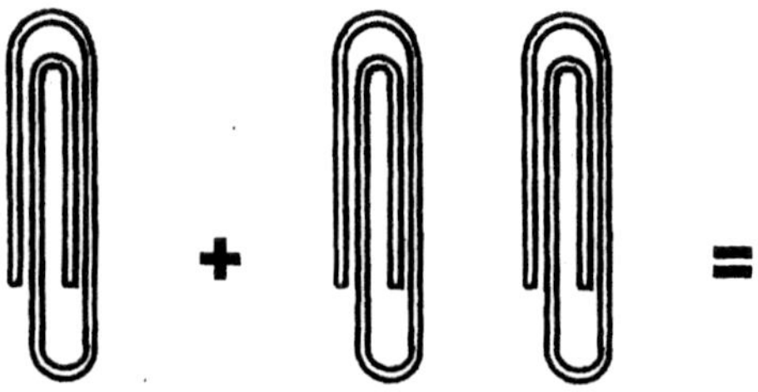

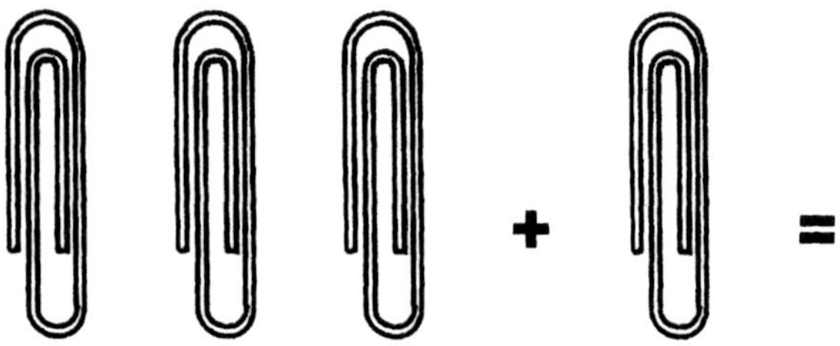

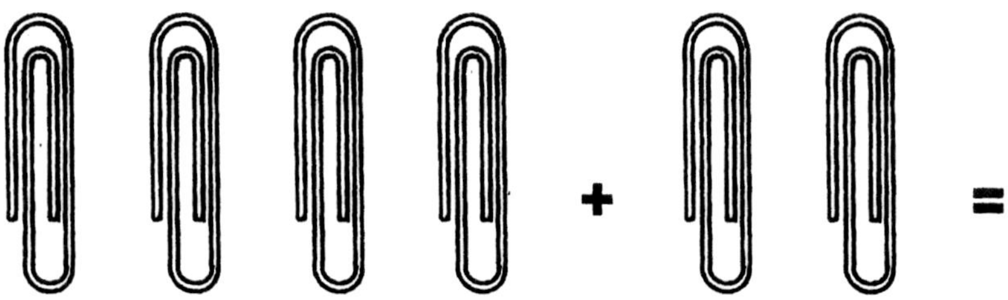

© Pearson Education, Inc. K

Name

Fishing Fun

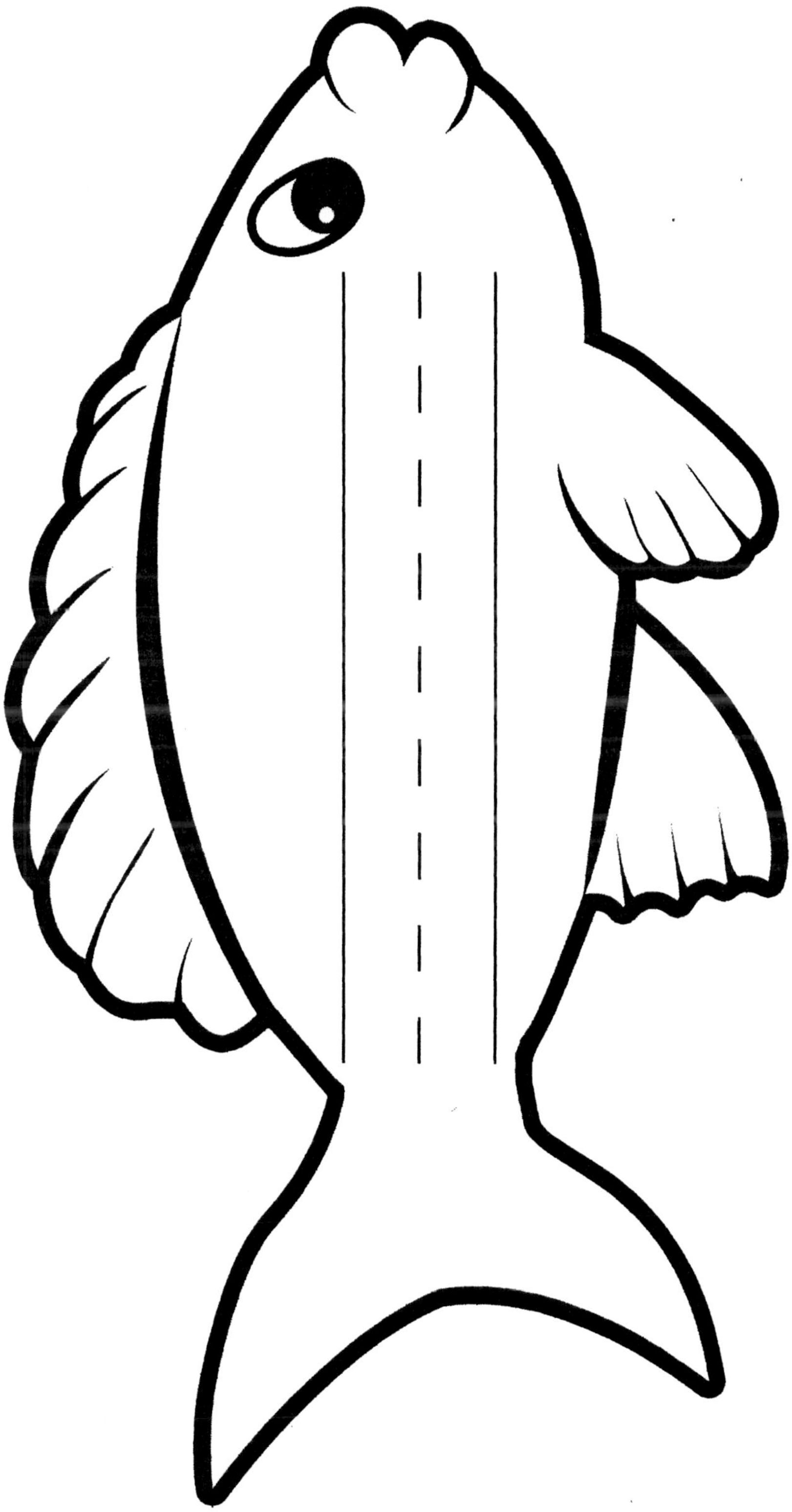

© Pearson Education, Inc. K

Name

Nonliving or Living?

© Pearson Education, Inc. K

Name

Nonliving or Living?

Nonliving	Living

© Pearson Education, Inc. K

Name ______________________

Number of Things

How Many?

______________ 

______________ 

______________ 

______________ 

______________ 

______________ 

© Pearson Education, Inc. K

Name ______________________________

Shapes on a Graph

Count the shapes and fill in the graph.

10				
9				
8				
7				
6				
5				
4				
3				
2				
1				
	○	□	△	▭

© Pearson Education, Inc. K

Name

Touch It!

It is a ______________________.

© Pearson Education, Inc. K

Name

How Do Plants Grow?

© Pearson Education, Inc. K

Name ______________________

Measure Plants

______ **paper clips**	______ **paper clips**	______ **paper clips**

© Pearson Education, Inc. K

Parts of a Plant

Parts of a Plant

Name ________________

1

Roots

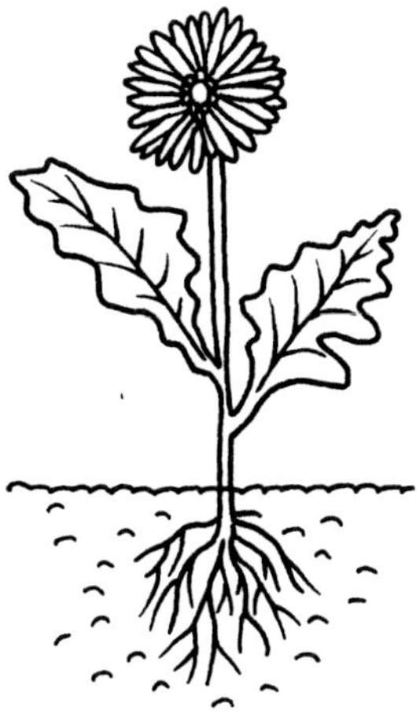

The roots of the plant take in water and hold the plant in the ground.

2

Stem

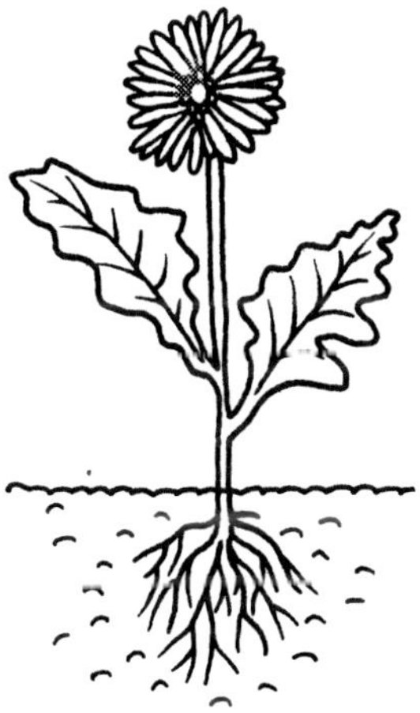

The stem carries the water up through the plant.

3

Leaves

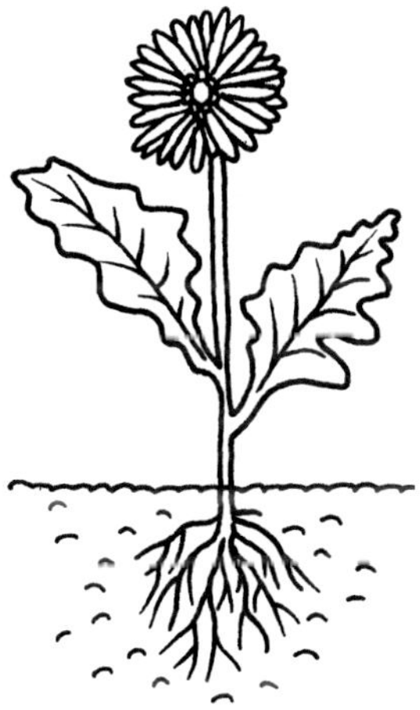

The leaves take in sunlight which the plant uses to make food.

4

Flower

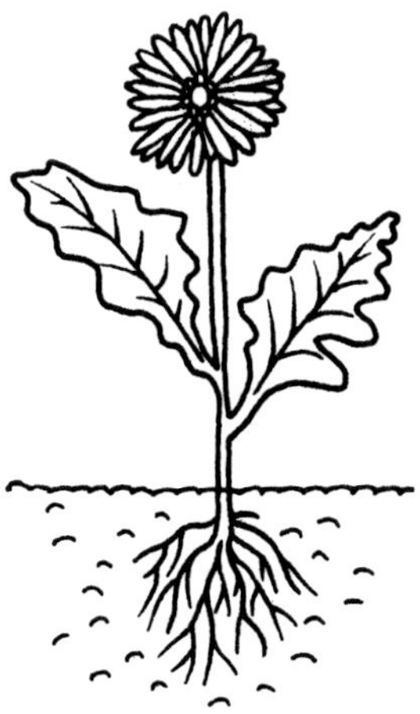

The flower produces seeds. Most flowers are bright and colorful.

5

My flower and me!

6

© Pearson Education, Inc. K

Name ______________________

What Is It?

It is red.
It is round.
It tastes good.
What is it?

It is green.
It has vegetables in it.
It is good for you.
What is it?

It is white.
It is best cold.
It comes from a cow.
What is it?

It is yellow.
It grows on a cob.
You eat it in the summer.
What is it?

© Pearson Education, Inc. K

Name

Where Is It?

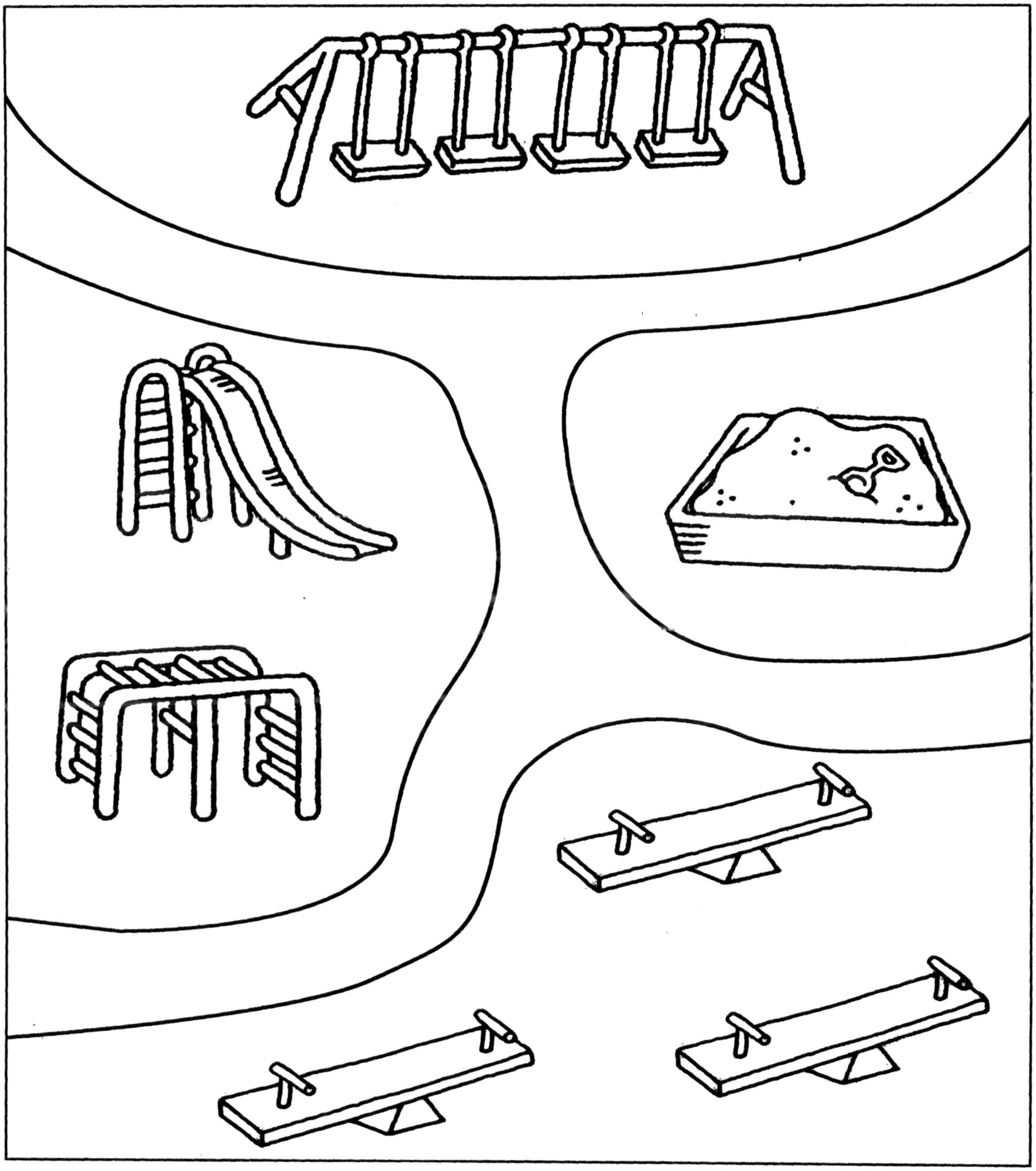

© Pearson Education, Inc. K

Name ______________________

Recycle or Not?

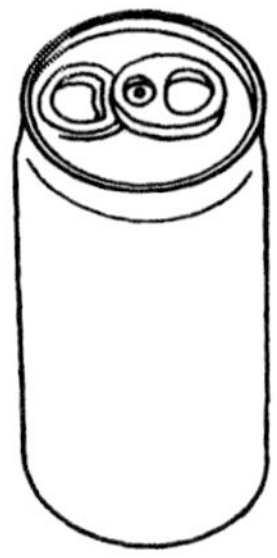

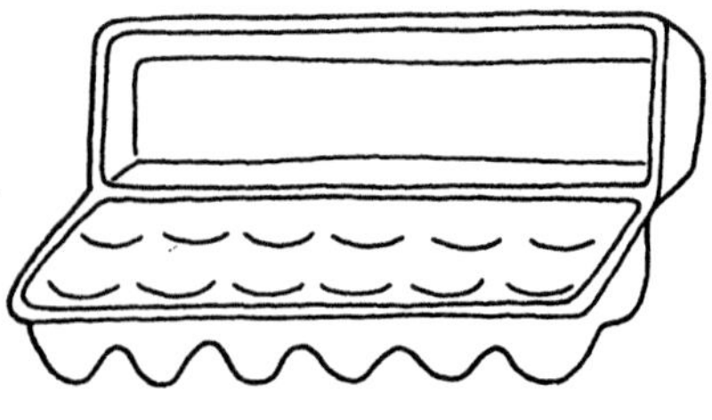

© Pearson Education, Inc. K

Name

Recycle or Not?

Recycle	Can't Recycle

© Pearson Education, Inc. K

Name ______________________

Reuse It!

© Pearson Education, Inc. K

Name

Four Seasons

fall	summer
winter	spring

© Pearson Education, Inc. K

Name ____________________

Winter or Summer?

Winter 	Summer 

© Pearson Education, Inc. K

Name

Spring Ducklings

© Pearson Education, Inc. K

Name ______________________________

Our Five Senses

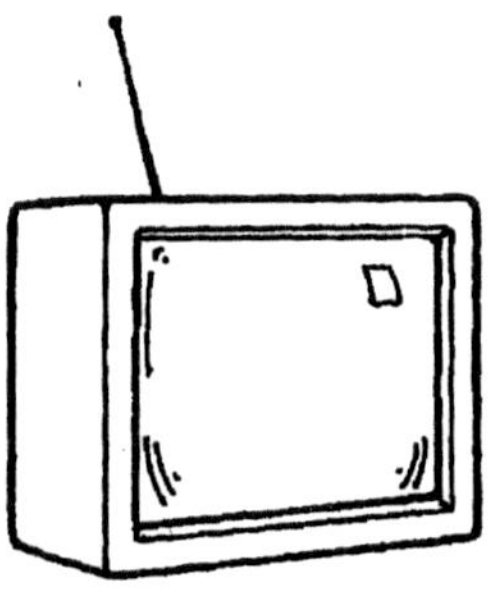

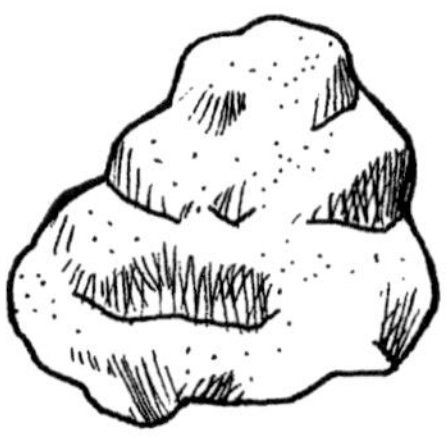

see

smell

touch

hear

taste

© Pearson Education, Inc. K

Name ______________________

Senses for Safety

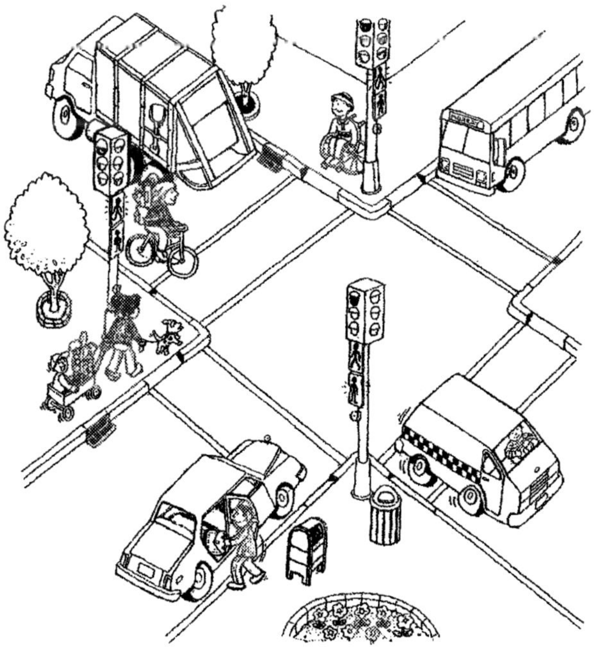

© Pearson Education, Inc. K

Name ______________________

Using My Senses

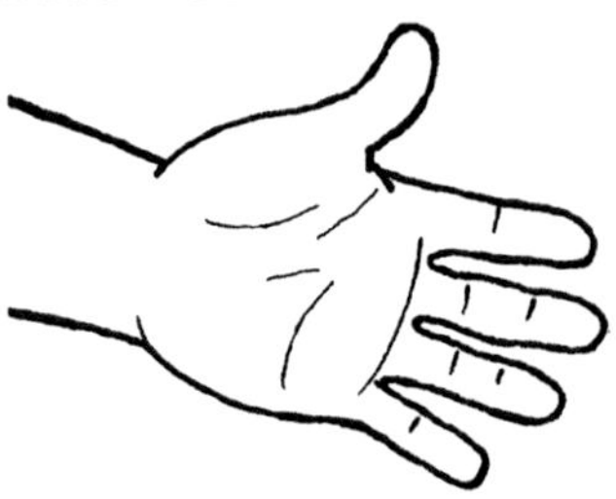	

© Pearson Education, Inc. K

Name ______________________

The Planets

3 Earth

8 Neptune

6 Saturn

2 Venus

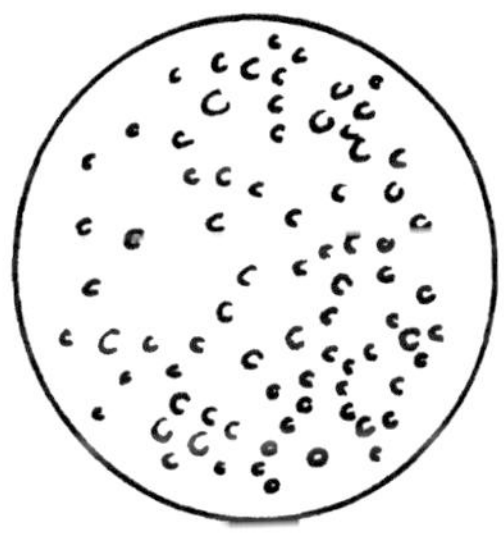

1 Mercury

4 Mars

5 Jupiter

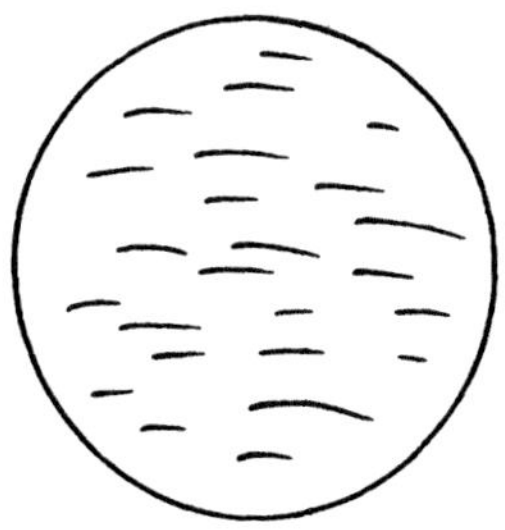

7 Uranus

© Pearson Education, Inc. K

Name

Astronauts

© Pearson Education, Inc. K

Name

Kinds of Land

mountain | valley | plain

© Pearson Education, Inc. K

Name

Animals of the Plains

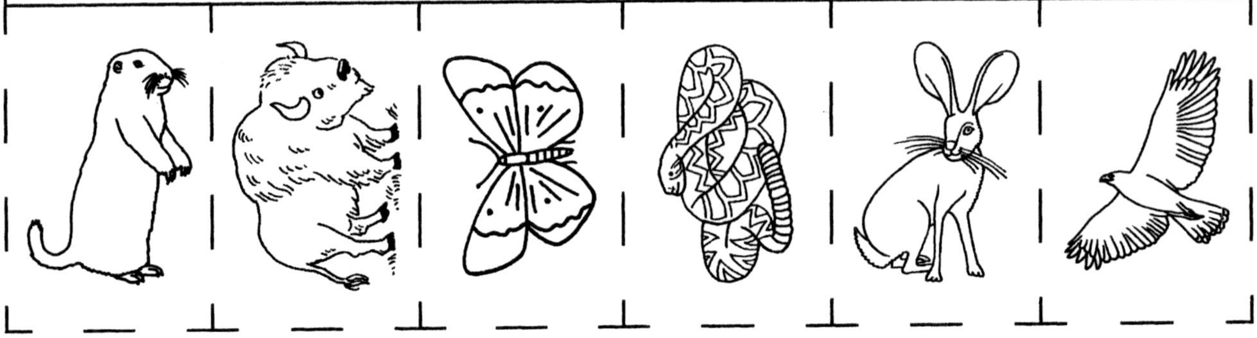

© Pearson Education, Inc. K

Name ______________________

Weather Watch

Day	Weather
Monday	
Tuesday	
Wednesday	
Thursday	
Friday	

© Pearson Education, Inc. K

Name ______________________

The Weather Report

Today is ______________________.

sunny **rainy** **cloudy**

windy **snowy**

© Pearson Education, Inc. K

Name

X-tra Special X rays

© Pearson Education, Inc. K

Name ______________________________

My Bones

My Book About Bones

Name ____________________

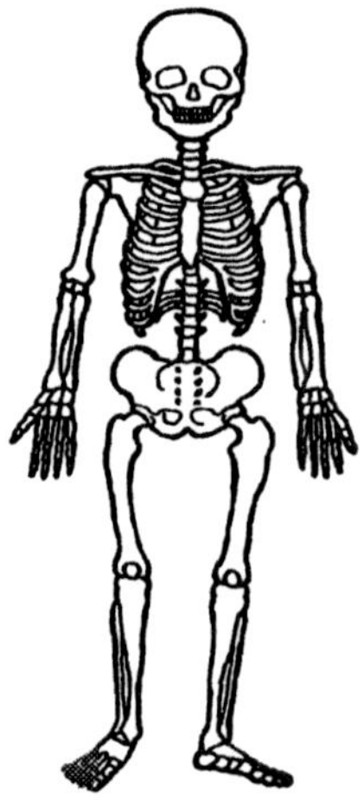

I have

____

bones in
my body.

My ears have

____

bones.

My legs have

____

bones.

Some

____

are protectors.

When I run and jump, I

thank my ____________.

© Pearson Education, Inc. K

Name

Making Shadows

© Pearson Education, Inc. K

Name ________________________

What Has a Shadow?

plastic wrap

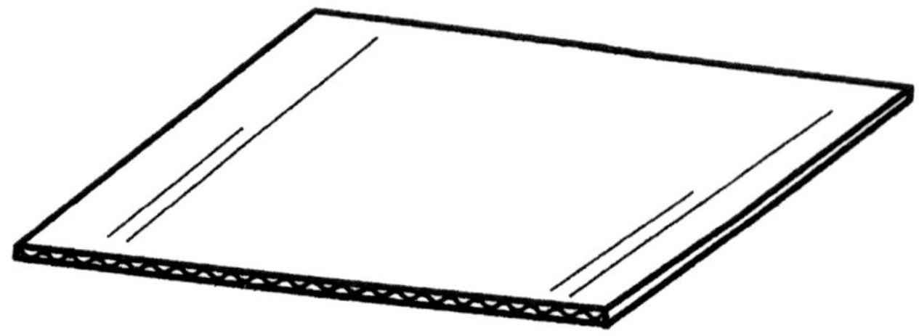

cardboard

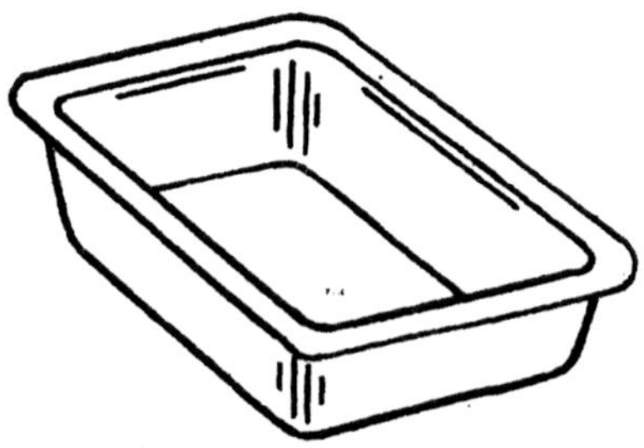

metal pan

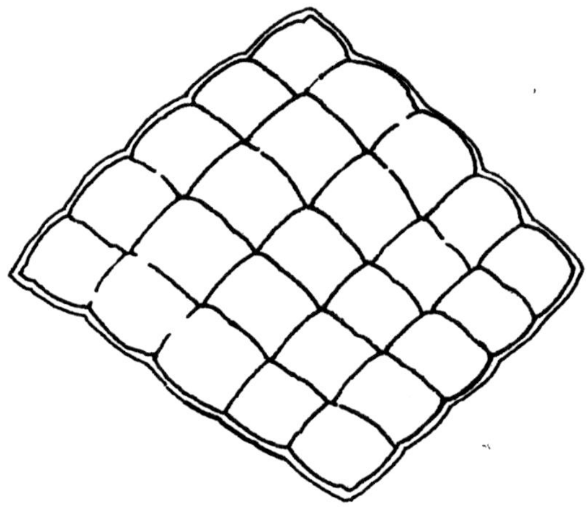

blanket

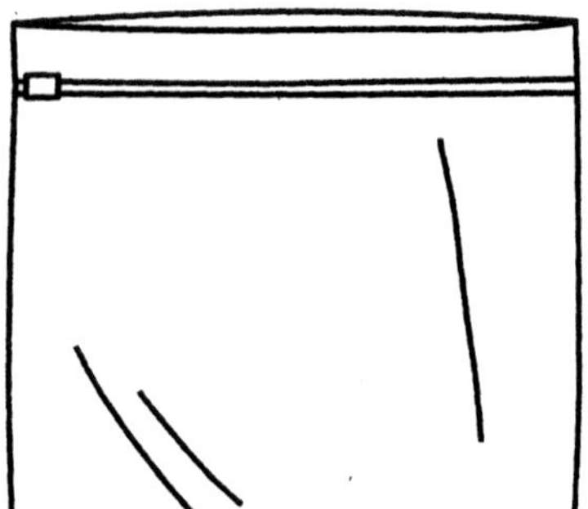

baggie

wood

© Pearson Education, Inc. K

Name

Who's at a Zoo?

© Pearson Education, Inc. K

Name

Zoo Animal Count

© Pearson Education, Inc. K

Name

What Animals Need

Animal	Water	Food	Shelter
dog			

Answers will vary but may include: cat—water dish, food dish, large pillow; horse—water trough, bale of hay, barn

80

Name

My Favorite Animal

This is a ________.

Answers will vary but may include: horse, cat, dog, elephant, or penguin.

81

Name

Animals Around the World

Answers will vary but may include: elephant, monkey, fish, or wolf.

rain forest grassland desert
tundra ocean forest

82

Name

Name That Body Part

head

arm

leg

83

Name

A Healthy Body

1. Get Exercise

2. Eat Right

3. Keep Clean

84

Name

Tell About Me

I ________.

Names and pictures will vary.

85

© Pearson Education, Inc. K

Name

A Butterfly's Life

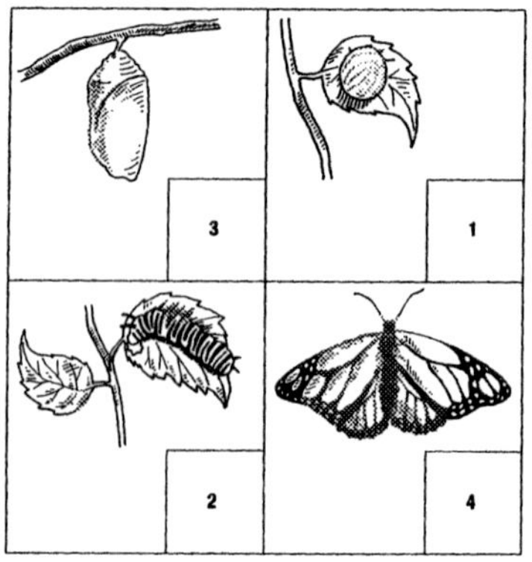

86

Name

Change and Grow

Then

Answers will vary but may include: crawled, cried, used a bottle.

Then I ______.

Now

Answers will vary but may include: run, jump, talk, drink from a glass.

Now I ______.

87

Name

Little to Big

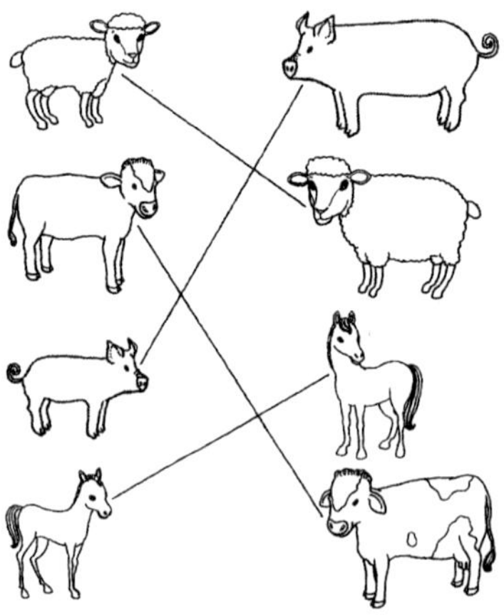

88

Name

Day to Night, Night to Day

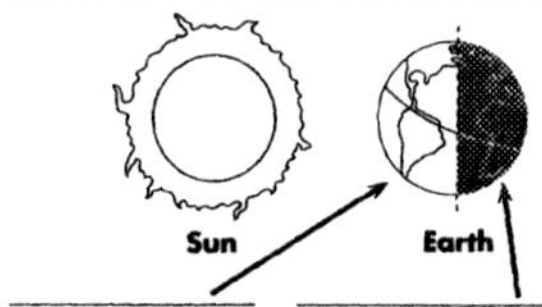

day night

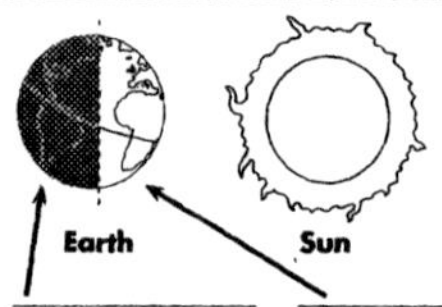

night day

89

Name

Day or Night?

Pictures will vary.

Sun Moon clouds
dark stars light

90

Name

Day Sky, Night Sky

In the day sky

I see ______.

Answers will vary but may include: Sun, clouds, blue sky.

In the night sky

I see ______.

Answers will vary but may include: stars, Moon, dark sky.

91

© Pearson Education, Inc. K

Name

Wonderful, Marvelous Dirt!

Pictures will vary.

92

Name

Earthworms

The Story of ____________'s Worm	This is my worm. Its name is ____________
My worm likes to ____________ on rainy days.	My worm helps flowers and plants to grow.

Answers will vary.

93

Name

Earth Rocks!

Color Color 4	1
Color 2	Color 4
Color 1	Color Color 3

94

Name

Is It Fast or Slow?

Fast	Slow
Answers will vary but may include: a car, a train, an airplane.	**Answers will vary but may include: a ball, a hot-air balloon, a child walking.**

95

Name

Is It Loud or Soft?

Loud	Soft

96

Name

Which Is Faster?

97

© Pearson Education, Inc. K

Name

What Is It?

Gas	Liquid	Solid
balloon	waterfall	wood block

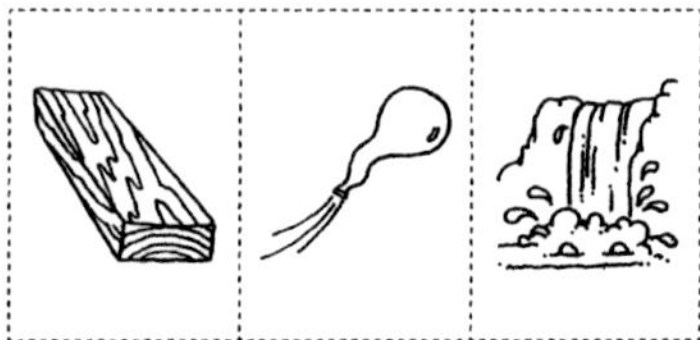

98

Name

Watch the Changes!

From Liquid (water) Children draw picture of water.	→	**To Solid (ice)** Children draw picture of ice cube.
From Solid (ice) Children draw picture of ice cubes.	→	**To Liquid (water)** Children draw picture of melted ice cubes.
From Liquid (water) Children draw picture of water.	→	**To Gas (water vapor)** Children draw picture of steam from teapot.

99

Name

All Steamed Up

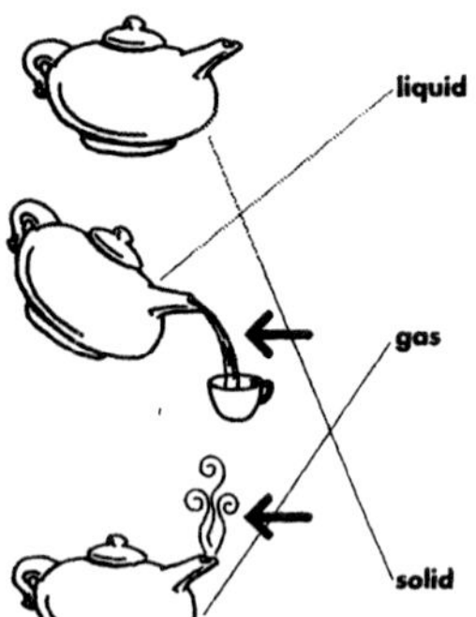

100

Name

Heat and Light

Heat
Answers will vary: picture of heater, fire, stove, or sun.
Light
Answers will vary: picture of lamp, flashlight, candle, or sun.

101

Name

The Sun

The Sun is...

Answers will vary but may include: a star, hot, round.

102

Name

Write a Rhyme

Where is the heat?

It is by my feet.

Look at the light.

It is so bright!

103

© Pearson Education, Inc. K

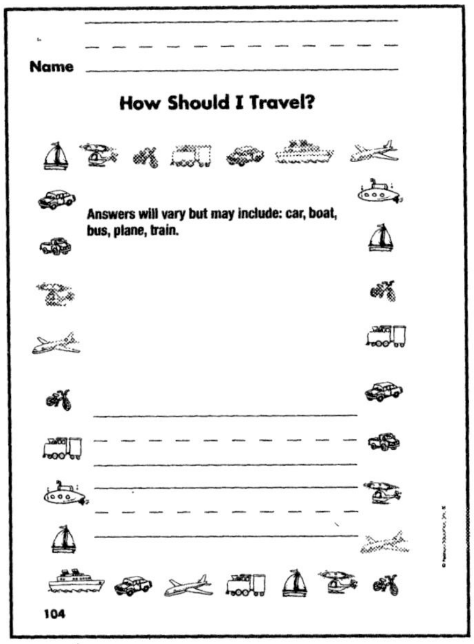
Name

How Should I Travel?

Answers will vary but may include: car, boat, bus, plane, train.

104

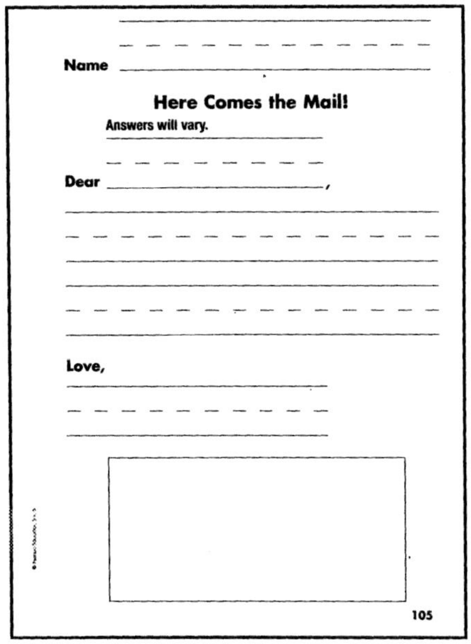
Name

Here Comes the Mail!

Answers will vary.

Dear ,

Love,

105

Name

Ways to Move

She jumps. She runs.

He hops. He walks.

She skips. She twirls.

He marches. He slides.

106

Name

Action Words

Answers will vary but may include: jump, run, walk, swim, hop.

107

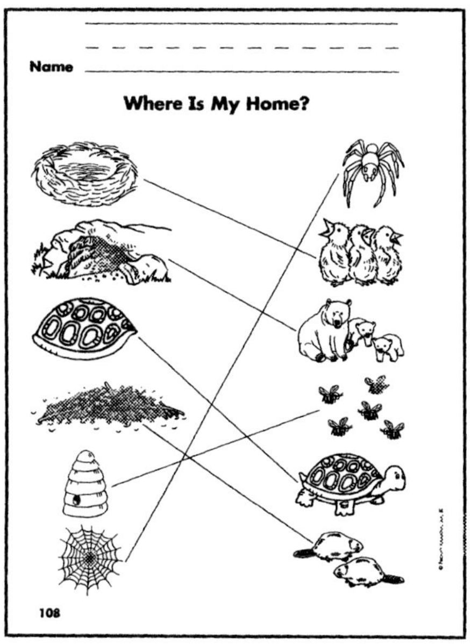
Name

Where Is My Home?

108

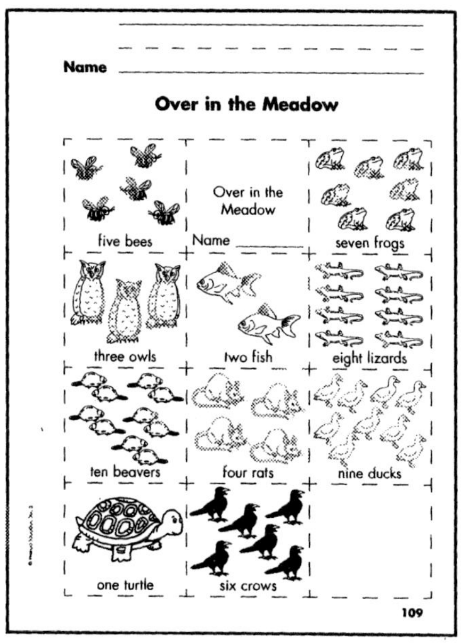
Name

Over in the Meadow

five bees	Over in the Meadow Name	seven frogs
three owls	two fish	eight lizards
ten beavers	four rats	nine ducks
one turtle	six crows	

109

© Pearson Education, Inc. K

Name

Finger Puppets

110

Name

Simple Machines

wheel	pulley	ramp	lever

111

Name

Wheel Count

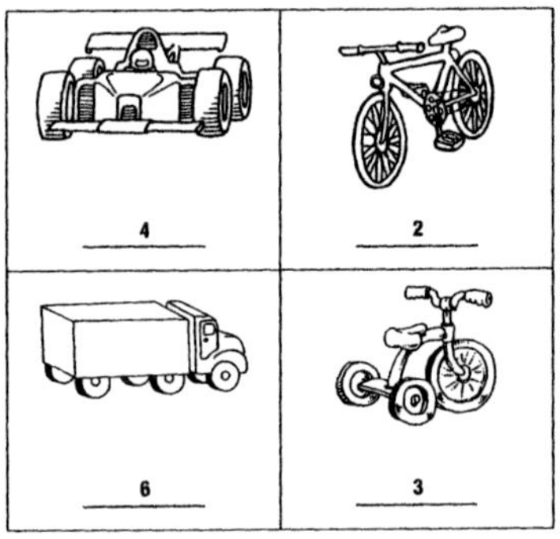

112

Name

Finish the Words

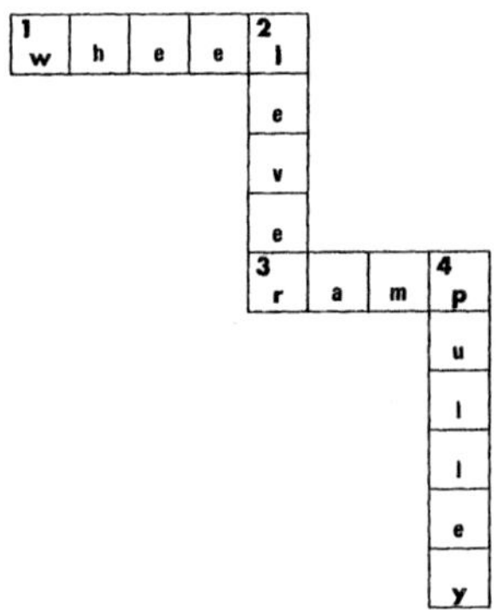

1. goes 'round and 'round
2. looks like a long stick
3. always at a tilt
4. needs a rope, a string, or a chain

113

Name

Magnetic Math

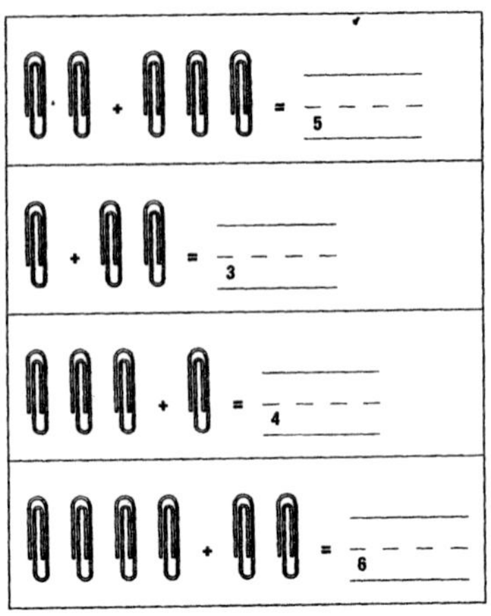

114

Name

Fishing Fun

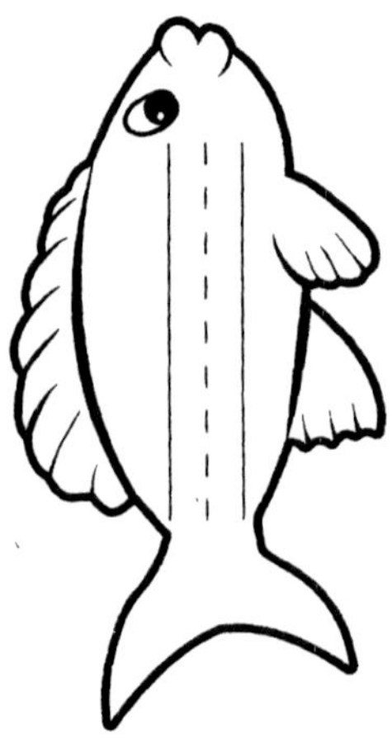

115

© Pearson Education, Inc. K

Name

Nonliving or Living?

Name

Nonliving or Living?

Nonliving 	Living 
Answers: table doll tricycle swing set	Answers: boy dog flower tree

Name

Number of Things

How Many?

1 ______

2 ______

3 ______

4 ______

5 ______

6 ______

Name

Shapes on a Graph

Count the shapes and fill in the graph.

10				
9				
8				
7				
6				
5		Answers will vary.		
4				
3				
2				
1				
	○	□	△	▭

Name

Touch It!

Answers will vary but may include: stuffed toys, bumpy sponge, ribbon, block.

It is a ______.

Name

How Do Plants Grow?

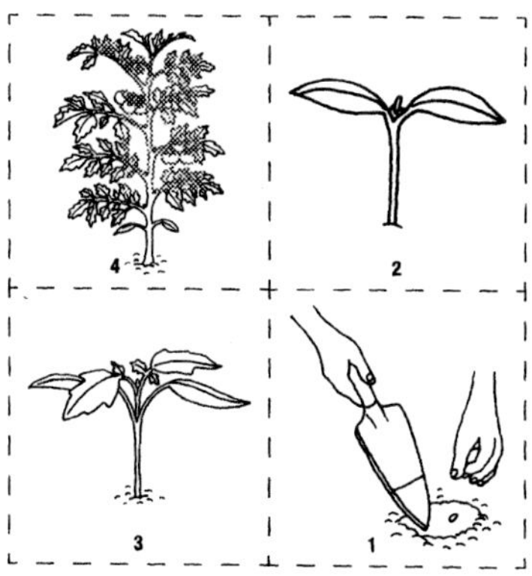

© Pearson Education, Inc. K

Name

Measure Plants

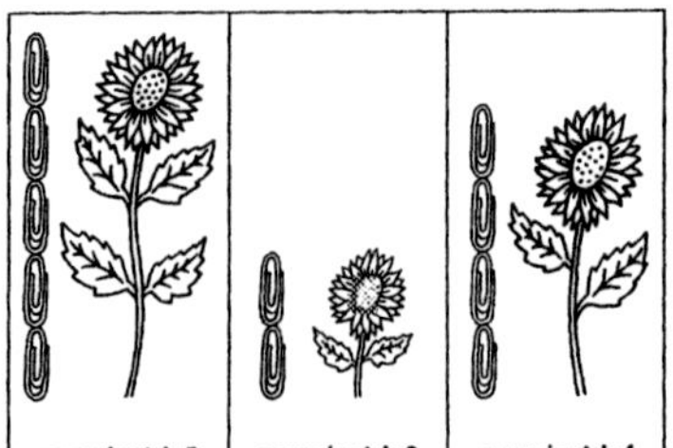

approximately 5 paper clips	approximately 2 paper clips	approximately 4 paper clips

Parts of a Plant

Parts of a Plant

Name

1

Roots

The roots of the plant take in water and hold the plant in the ground.

2

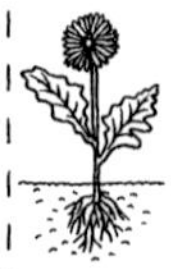

Stem

The stem carries the water up through the plant.

3

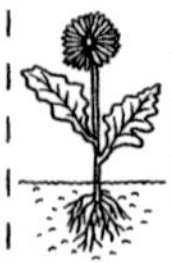

Leaves

The leaves take in sunlight which the plant uses to make food.

4

Flower

The flower produces seeds. Most flowers are bright and colorful.

5

My flower and me!

6

Name

What Is It?

It is red.
It is round.
It tastes good.
What is it?

color

It is green.
It has vegetables in it.
It is good for you.
What is it?

color

It is white.
It is best cold.
It comes from a cow.
What is it?

color

It is yellow.
It grows on a cob.
You eat it in the summer.
What is it?

color

Name

Where Is It?

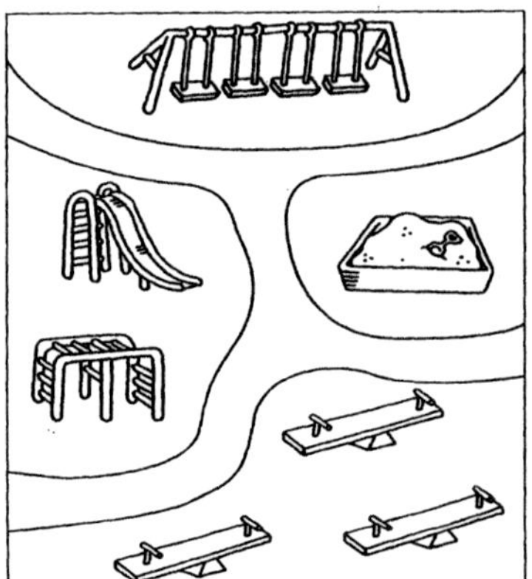

color swings blue, color slide green, color the sandbox red, circle the seesaws in blue, circle the monkey bars in green

Name

Recycle or Not?

Name

Recycle or Not?

Recycle	Can't Recycle
milk cartons	flower
newspaper	stuffed teddy bear
empty egg carton	tape
soda pop can	pillow

© Pearson Education, Inc. K

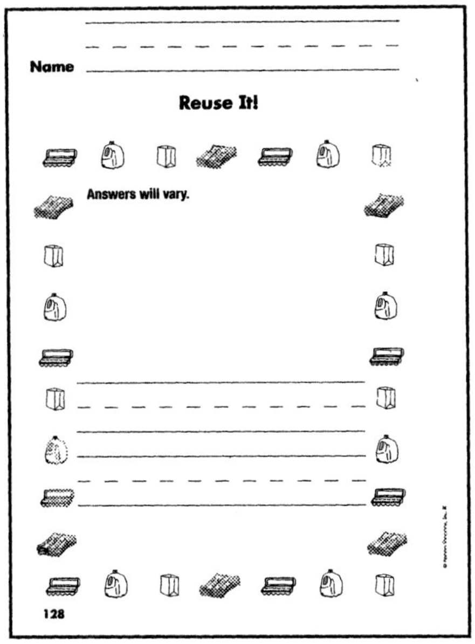
Name

Reuse It!

Answers will vary.

128

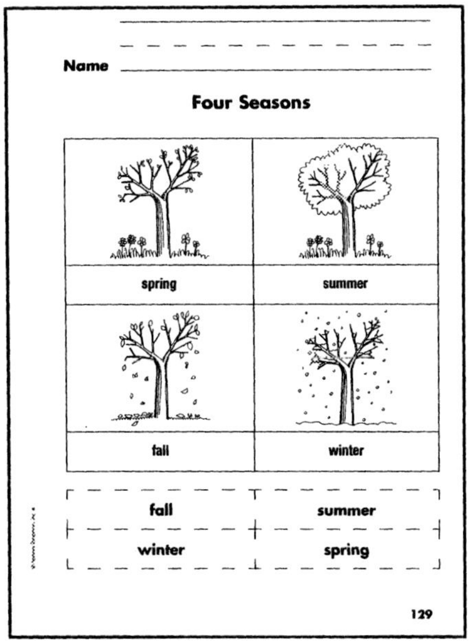
Name

Four Seasons

spring	summer
fall	winter

fall	summer
winter	spring

129

Name

Winter or Summer?

Winter	Summer
Summer	Winter
Winter	Winter
Summer	Summer
Winter	Summer

130

Name

Spring Ducklings

2	3
1	4

131

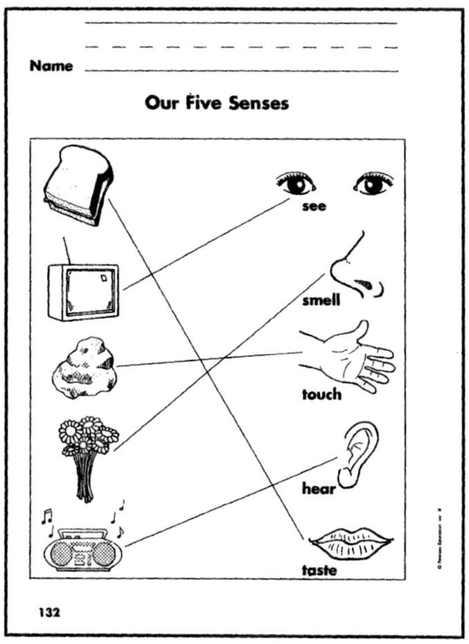
Name

Our Five Senses

see

smell

touch

hear

taste

132

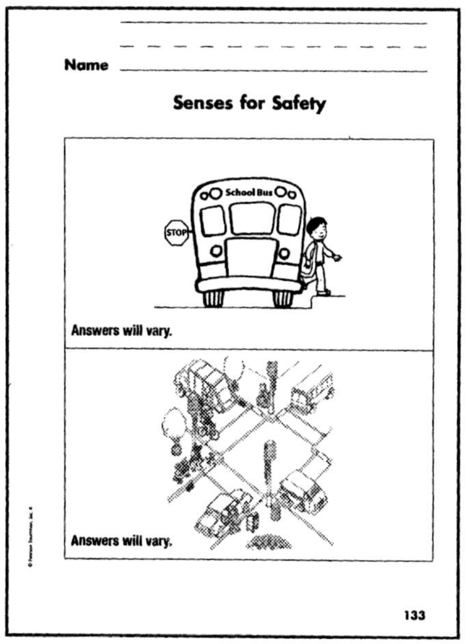
Name

Senses for Safety

Answers will vary.

Answers will vary.

133

© Pearson Education, Inc. K

Name

Using My Senses

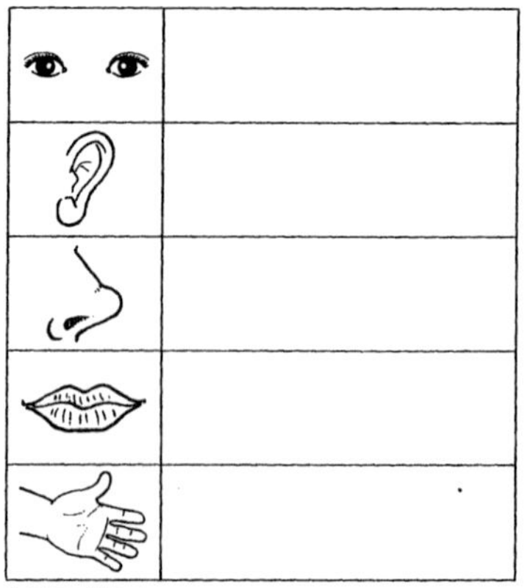

Answers will vary.

134

Name

The Planets

3 Earth	8 Neptune	6 Saturn
2 Venus	1 Mercury	4 Mars
5 Jupiter	7 Uranus	

Planets are to be put in order using the numbers.

135

Name

Astronauts

136

Name

Kinds of Land

valley

plain

mountain

mountain	valley	plain

137

Name

Animals of the Plains

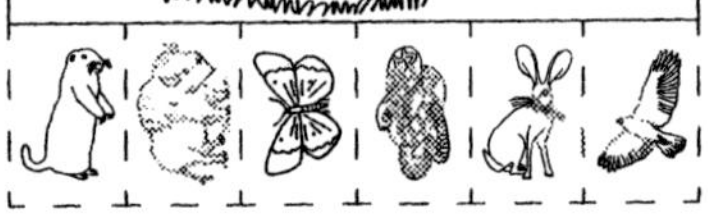

138

Name

Weather Watch

Answers will vary.

Day	Weather
Monday	
Tuesday	
Wednesday	
Thursday	
Friday	

139

© Pearson Education, Inc. K

Name

The Weather Report

Answers will vary.

Today is ______.

sunny rainy cloudy

windy snowy

140

Name

X-tra Special X rays

Pictures will vary.

141

Name

My Bones

Pictures will vary.

My Book About Bones Name ______	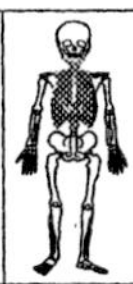 I have 206 bones in my body.
 My ears have small bones.	 My legs have big bones.
 Some bones are protectors.	 When I run and jump, I thank my bones.

142

Name

Making Shadows

143

Name

What Has a Shadow?

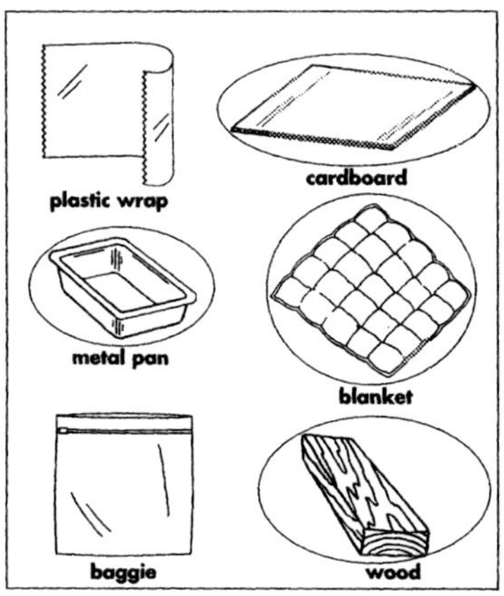

144

Name

Who's at a Zoo?

145

© Pearson Education, Inc. K

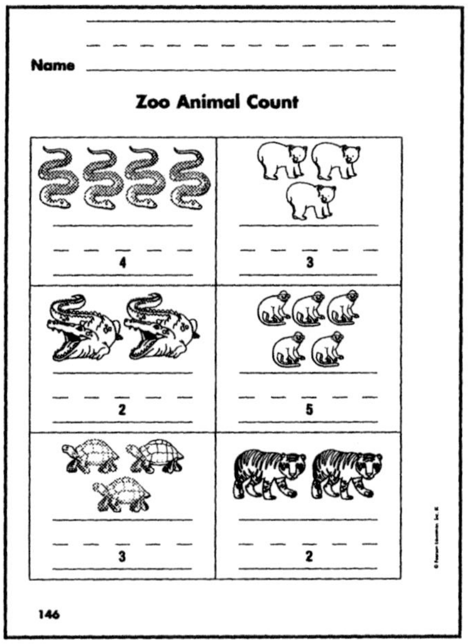
Name

Zoo Animal Count

4	3
2	5
3	2

146

© Pearson Education, Inc. K